A People's Courage

Civil resistance in German-occupied Italy

By FILIPPO IERANÒ

Published by The Monte San Martino Trust, 2022

ISBN 978-0-9576102-2-4

Translated by Anne Bewicke-Copley, Letitia Blake,
Christine English and John Simkins

Table of contents

PART ONE

Preface to the English edition

This book is a translation into English of Antigone nella Valle del Tenna by the Italian historian Filippo Ieranò, which was first published in 2003 by the Regional Council of Le Marche. The English version is a translation of the second Italian edition, issued in 2017. The Monte San Martino Trust is extremely grateful to Professor Ieranò for granting us publication rights.

Since its foundation in 1989 the Trust has collated and made available to the public nearly 200 memoirs written by Allied servicemen who escaped from Italian prisoner of war camps following the Armistice with Italy in September 1943. The soldiers, who were on the run from Italian fascists and the occupying German army, often owed their lives to peasant families living in the mountains. These families, the *contadini*, offered their help at great risk to their own lives and were prepared to share what little they had with the escapers.

Despite its efforts, the Trust holds few accounts by the *contadini* of their own experiences. It was this lack that prompted us to make Ieranò's book available to English readers. The witness statements that he collected, and which comprise Part Three of his book, are not only rare; they give invaluable insight into the motives of the *contadini* in defying authority.

Ieranò carried out these interviews in the Tenna Valley, in Le Marche, between 1999 and 2002. His subjects were very elderly, having been children at the time that their families hosted an escaper. This translation has attempted to retain the conversational speech of the interviewees, without smoothing out the colloquialisms that give an immediacy to their recollections.

The PoWs would have fled from one of the three camps in the region, in particular the camp at Servigliano, which is itself in the Tenna Valley. Quite apart from describing the hair-raising circumstances, with the likelihood of discovery never far away, the interviews shine a light on the still-feudal life of these poor families, who were living hand-to-mouth. The final testimony, which is as harrowing as any, describes the plight of a Jewish family oppressed by Italy's anti-racial legislation.

In Part Two of the book Ieranò sets out the historical background: the Armistice with Italy; the fall of Mussolini; the resistance of the German army to the advance up Italy by the Allies; and the round-ups by the Germans and fascists to hunt down Italian partisans and escaped Allied prisoners. He also addresses different aspects of the relationship between helper family and escaper, citing the witness statements that comprise Part Three.

A central thesis of Ieranò's book is that the resilience of the *contadini* in defying the fascist dictatorship amounted to passive resistance, an action every bit as valid and commendable as the military resistance of the partisans. It was for this reason that Ieranò chose to reference Antigone in the Italian title. In Sophocles's play, Antigone defies Creon, the Theban ruler, and in doing so breaks an unjust law. Ieranò maintains that the *contadini* were doing the same.

We hope that you enjoy this book and wish to support the work of the Monte San Martino Trust in acknowledging the brave Italians who rescued escaped prisoners of war. The Trust depends entirely upon donations to carry out its work, which includes granting language study bursaries in England to Italians aged 18 to 25. It also promotes academic research into the Allied presence in Italy during the Second World War.

Anne Bewicke-Copley, Letitia Blake, Christine English and John Simkins, on behalf of the Monte San Martino Trust
www.msmtrust.org.uk
info@msmtrust.org.uk

Glossary

The Allies: A military coalition formed during the Second World War to oppose the Axis powers led by Germany, Japan and Italy. The Allies' principal members were the UK, USA, Soviet Union and China.

The Armistice: In effect, Italy's surrender. This was signed on 3 September 1943 and made public on 8 September. Italy ceased to be an ally of the occupying German army.

Carabinieri: Italian national police force, organised as a military unit.

Contadini: Italian term for subsistence farmers, who worked under a system known as *mezzadria*, meaning "half and half". They had to give half of their produce to their landlord.

Le Marche: Region in eastern central Italy.

Nazi-Fascists: Italian term describing fascists who supported Germany's Nazi regime.

PoW: Prisoner of war.

Republic of Salò: Formally known as the Italian Social Republic, this was a puppet state under the Germans set up under Benito Mussolini in the later stages of the war.

Republican: Spelt with a capital R, a pejorative term mocking a supporter of the Italian Social Republic.

The Resistance: Spelt with a capital R, this was the partisan resistance movement formed to oppose German occupation militarily.

Wanted!

The Italian text below comprised a poster issued by the occupying German authorities warning of retribution should anybody aid an escaped prisoner of war or member of the Resistance.

Lotta contro il favoreggiamento del nemico

☐ TACETE tutto quanto vedete e udite intorno a voi delle Truppe Germaniche. Se, ad esempio, il nemico verrà a sapere che nel vostro paese ci sono truppe tedesche il vostro paese sarà bombardato dal nemico senza pietà. Tacendo salverete il vostro paese, la vostra casa, i vostri beni.

☐ SEGNALATE ai comandi tedeschi ogni prigioniero di guerra evaso, ogni spia o sabotatore e ogni persona colpevole di attentato contro i soldati: segnalate pure i preparativi di attentato, sabotaggio e spionaggio.

☐ AVRETE UN PREMIO di Lire 1,800 per ogni prigioniero, sabotatore ecc. . . . catturato in seguito alla vostra segnalazione.

☐ SEGNALATE ai comandi tedeschi ogni apparecchio radio trasmittente.

☐ AVRETE UN PREMIO di Lire 5,000 per ogni apparecchio segreto rintracciato in seguito alla vostra segnalazione.

☐ Sarà PUNITO secondo le severe leggi germaniche di guerra, eventualmente CON LA MORTE, chi tralascerà le persone e i fatti suddetti, chi aiuterà tali persone con vitto, alloggio o vestiario, e chi ne faciliterà la fuga.

☐ SEVERI PROVVEDIMENTI saranno presi contro gli abitanti del paese se la presenza o il transito di prigionieri evasi o di spie, sabotatori ecc. . . . . non saranno segnalati tempestivamente dalla popolazione.

☐ Il presente manifesto deve essere affisso sulla porta di tutti i pubblici edifici e di tutte le chiese, a scanso di severi provvedimenti contro i responsabili della mancata affissione e contro chi arbitrariamente staccherà un manifesto.

Il comandante delle Truppe Germaniche

Fight against aiding and abetting the enemy

☐ KEEP SILENT regarding everything you see and hear around you about the German troops. If, for example, the enemy learns that there are German troops in your village, your village will be bombed by the enemy without mercy. By keeping silent you will save your village, your home, and your possessions.

☐ REPORT to the German commanders every escaped prisoner of war, every spy or saboteur and every person responsible for an attack on the soldiers: also report any preparations for attack, sabotage and espionage.

Filippo Ieranò

☐ YOU WILL HAVE A REWARD of Lire 1,800 for each prisoner, saboteur, etc. captured following your report.

☐ REPORT any radio transmitting device to the German commandos.

☐ YOU WILL HAVE A REWARD of Lire 5,000 for each secret device traced following your report.

☐ Whoever fails to report the aforementioned persons and facts, or helps such persons with food, accommodation or clothing, or facilitates their escape, WILL BE PUNISHED according to the strict Germanic laws of war, even WITH DEATH.

☐ SEVERE MEASURES will be taken against the inhabitants of the village if the presence or the transit of escaped prisoners or spies, saboteurs, etc. . . . is not promptly reported by the population.

☐ This notice must be posted on the door of all public buildings and churches. Otherwise there will be severe measures against those responsible for the failure to post it and against anyone who arbitrarily detaches the notice.

The commander of the German troops

PART TWO

The title

Antigone is the title of a tragedy by Sophocles, performed for the first time in Athens in 442 BC. It tells the story of the sacrifice of Antigone, the daughter of Oedipus. In order to bury her brother, Polynice, she defies the prohibition of the king of Thebes, Creon, and pays with her life for her audacity in disobeying a law that she considers unjust. The story illustrates the deep anxieties that beset every man who finds himself confronted with the exercise of power devoid of moral foundations; anxieties that manifest themselves in the clash between the heart and the mind, between piety and indifference to religion, between conscience and blind obedience to the narrow-minded authoritarianism of a tyrant. The character of Antigone becomes a paradigm of civil disobedience.

Curiously, this model was acted out, albeit in a different way, by the people of the Tenna Valley in Italy's central eastern region of Le Marche. In these pages, the ordinary men and women of the valley relate events that took place during the civil resistance to fascism. Between September 1943 and June 1944 they exhibited courage and a sense of justice by aiding Allied servicemen and Jews who had escaped from Servigliano prisoner of war camp, thereby disregarding dire threats made by the Nazi-Fascists.

Of course, the character of Antigone, now more than 2,000 years old, also recalls other rebellions and acts of resistance, other searches for freedom and justice. One simply has to substitute the agents of the Soviet KGB or the soldiers of Pinochet for the fascists in these stories. Or, if not them, the agents of the many powerful men who throughout history have violated human rights and used brutal methods while denying people their dignity.

The dialogue between Antigone and Creon

Creon: You there, whose head is drooping to the ground,
Do you admit this or deny you did it?
Antigone: I say I did it and I don't deny it.
Creon: . . . tell me not at length but in a word.
You knew the order not to do this thing?
Antigone: I knew, of course I knew, the word was plain.
Creon: And still you dared to overstep these laws?
Antigone: For me it was not Zeus who made that order.
Nor did that Justice who lives with the gods below
mark out such laws to hold among mankind.
Nor did I think your orders were so powerful
that you, a mortal man, could over-run
the gods' unwritten and unfailing laws.
Not now, nor yesterday, they always live,
And no one knows their origin in time.
So not through fear of any man's proud spirit
would I be likely to neglect these laws,
draw on myself the gods' sure punishment.
I knew that I must die; how could I not
Even without your warning. If I die
Before my time, I say it is a gain. . . .

Introduction

This reprint [in 2017] of *Antigone nella Valle del Tenna* has some new aspects: there is a longer introduction, a thematic presentation, the addition of new witness statements and the theatrical adaptation of the first edition has been eliminated. The aim remains the same: to enable men and women to describe events that they themselves experienced. In this way an aspect of history comes to light that is rarely found in books, featuring protagonists who are simple people leading ordinary lives. The powerful are left in the background.

The facts narrated took place between September 1943 and June 1944. They do not belong, therefore, to the distant past but are still alive in the memories of the elderly, many of whom have been able to document them.

The events occurred in the middle Tenna Valley, at the centre of which was Servigliano prisoner of war camp. The place has lost its sinister aspect, given that in the 1970s the camp was dismantled and turned into a multi-sports centre. However, there are still visible remains, such as the high walls with glass shards, strands of rusty and twisted barbed wire and the ruins of the former infirmary.

In general, the historical period under study (only a few months) is rich in documentation, but probing personal memories of that harsh winter in the Tenna Valley is arguably a better way of revealing the humble, but incredibly brave, role played by simple, unknown people. Ultimately the intention is to highlight aspects of the resistance to Nazi-Fascism that historians have only started to consider in recent years. The facts can help

Filippo Ieranò

map out an educational path with which to promote peace and democracy.

Recourse to memory, for those who seek to understand the present, thus becomes an opportunity for cultural growth, to the benefit of every generation: adults can re-read their own history in a new way and the young can discover and comprehend the link between their own times and those of their grandparents.

On 10 July 1943 the Allied landing in Sicily provoked the crisis of the fascist regime. Defeat now seemed inevitable. Mussolini and his hierarchy saw that their plan for Italy to rank alongside Germany and other victors of the war as a future ruler of the world had failed. The strategy of "a handful of men to sacrifice", in that the war would be short and victorious, had turned into a catastrophe, with the deaths of hundreds of thousands of Italians, both soldiers and civilians.

The key moment of this political implosion occurred during the meeting of the Grand Council of Fascism on 25 July 1943. In an atmosphere of great tension, [Dino] Grandi's Order of the Day, which ousted Mussolini from the government, was approved. Immediately, King Victor Emmanuel III signed the Duce's arrest order. It looked as if fascism was finished: 20 years of harsh dictatorship were over. The king entrusted the government to Marshal [Pietro] Badoglio, who restored the freedoms granted by the Albertine Statute [of 1848]. In the following days, as an expression of long-repressed desire, spontaneous marches and demonstrations sprang up. In some towns, fascist headquarters were attacked and members of the hierarchy and fascist collaborators made themselves scarce.

Those who took part in the early demonstrations were the most politically motivated, the anti-fascists. But the size of the crowds and the varied locations enable us to identify a new set of actors, namely ordinary people discovering their democratic conscience. Not surprisingly, the most popular slogans were anti-war.

We should not fall into the error of concluding that the Badoglio government respected constitutional freedoms. On the contrary, Badoglio established an authoritarian government, formed mainly of military personnel who, in the confusion prevalent at the time, took decisions that made his political strategy clear: to counter possible action by anti-fascist groups or parties. In fact, on his orders, as soon as 26 July Gen. Mario Roatta [Chief of Staff of the Army] ordained that: ". . . anyone who committed acts of violence or rebellion against the armed forces and police, or uttered insults against them and the institutions, would immediately be shot. The circular also ordered that any military officer employed in public order who had given the slightest sign of solidarity with offenders against public order, or had disrespected his superiors or institutions, would be shot immediately. Assemblies of more than three people would be dispersed under arms and without prior notice or forewarning of any kind."[1]

These words give the sense that it was not the fascists who were the enemy to be controlled but rather the people who poured into the streets to affirm and celebrate their new-found freedom. They were words that started a bloodbath. As early as 28 July, during a workers' demonstration in Reggio Emilia, soldiers opened fire on the crowd, leaving nine dead. On the same day, at an anti-war demonstration in Bari, Italian soldiers again fired on the mob, killing nine people and wounding 40. By the end of July the number of dead had reached 83, with 308 wounded and more than 1,500 arrested. This severity and authoritarianism, however, could not prevent a political change that resembled a metamorphosis. The people had entered the political arena; they were no longer spectators but protagonists. And as the Allies brushed past Salerno, advancing up the peninsula to be constantly welcomed as liberators, Badoglio tried both to reassure the Germans about continuing the war at their side and to make a deal with the Allies that would not be considered a surrender and would guarantee a modicum of dignity for the Italian royal family.[2]

The Armistice was signed at Cassibile, near Syracuse, on 3 September, but Badoglio soon appeared uncertain. The Italian government's indecision in announcing the Armistice led the Allies to suspect some sort of change of heart and, in the face of this unexplained hesitation, they carried out new and heavy bombardments: on 5 September in Civitavecchia and Viterbo and on 6 September in Naples. Despite this, it was not the Italian government but the Allies who broke the silence and who, on the afternoon of 8 September, announced that the Armistice had been signed. One hour later Badoglio confirmed it on the radio.

The announcement sparked a renewed outbreak of enthusiasm. From north to south, everyone was convinced that, now peace had been made with the Allies, Italy was also out of the conflict. That was not the case! Italy was on the verge of becoming the scene not only of a violent clash between two armies, the Germans and the Allies, but also one between two political cultures, the fascism of the Italian Social Republic and the liberal-democracy of the National Liberation Committee (CLN).

In the hours immediately after the Armistice's announcement the Germans set up Operation Axis, which provided for the occupation of the entire peninsula. Meanwhile, Badoglio, part of the government and the Supreme Military Command, the king and some members of the royal family left Rome for the liberated city of Brindisi and put themselves under the protection of the Allies.

Their flight fractured the command structure and there were hours of confusion amid a power vacuum. The commanders of the various garrisons of the Italian army, left without clear orders, asked themselves what they should do: were the Germans still to be considered friends or regarded as enemies? And if they were enemies, should one fight them? As German divisions invaded Italy, Italian soldiers fell into the hands of German detachments. Italian units deployed in eastern Europe and in the Balkans found their predicament even more serious. Fighting alongside the Germans, or following a war strategy dictated by Berlin, landed them in chaos. Wherever Italian troops came into contact with German units they faced a choice: either to co-operate or be deported to the infamous labour camps in Germany.

Despite the nightmare of forced labour, only a tiny minority proved willing to join the army of the new-born Republic of Salò. Hundreds of thousands of soldiers deliberately chose the concentration camps. And others, as on the Greek island of Kefalonia, resisted the German army with the few means at their disposal and were slain in their thousands. There were also instances of mass desertion due to the confusion that reigned in barracks:

the soldiers threw down their arms and shed their uniforms, while heading for home on foot or by whichever means they could get hold of.

As all this was going on, tens of thousands of Allied prisoners escaped from prisoner of war camps, some of which had been abandoned by their guards, and thousands of Jews left their homes to avoid persecution by the Nazi-Fascists.

An astonishing number of people were on the move, crossing countryside and woods looking for places to hide in order to escape continual round-ups. The majority were aiming for the front line, which on the Adriatic side of the peninsular was considered to be in the vicinity of Pescara. Thousands of frightened people were compelled by hunger and hardship to seek food, shelter and companionship from people whom they did not know, especially the *contadini* [peasant farmers]. The size of this exodus is not easy to calculate but it is estimated that in the Fermano alone, the heart of Le Marche, more than 10,000 sought relief.

Italy was now divided into two: in the centre-north, occupied by the Germans, there was the Italian Social Republic; the south, occupied by the Allies, hosted the kingdom. The two governments faced each other, each under the rigid control of an occupying army. The soul of the country was now in the hands of ordinary people, who spontaneously breathed life into the liberation struggle, comprising both the armed Resistance movement of the partisans and unarmed resistance.

The testimonies collected here try to shed light on this second, unarmed, form of resistance. The events of 8 September, therefore, played a fundamental role in the rebirth of Italy, a watershed in the country's history.

A People's Courage

"Until it is clear that 8 September, whatever the mistakes and responsibilities of the political and military leadership concerning the Armistice, did not resolve Italy's crisis but instead reflected the moral standing of the vast majority of Italians, it will not be possible to understand its true nature, scope, or consequence. The same applies to its role in the events of the following two years and also in the post-war period. And also today, which in a sense is even more important."[3]

The facts retold in these pages certainly relate to the diverse phenomenon known as the Resistance, a term commonly understood as participation in political, moral and military opposition to Nazi-Fascism. However, to understand how the Resistance was represented post-war we must refer to a decree law, the Ministry of Defence's *Decreto Legge Luogoteneziale* of 21 August 1945, n. 518. This only recognised as "partisan" those who had been part of organised groups and had participated in at least three armed actions. The primacy of armed and organised resistance was underlined. Other individuals who had in their different ways opposed Nazi-Fascism were given no credit.

In contrast, the stories in this book are an invitation to reconsider the issue, because the logic of that decree law has served to marginalise the role and function of thousands of "non-armed" resisters. Even at today's celebratory ceremonies the focus is always on the courage, suffering and sacrifice of those who fought for freedom by taking up arms. But those who spontaneously carried out unarmed civil disobedience, contributing to the collapse of fascism, are greeted with silence, a silence that increasingly descends into the darkness of history. These people, too, showed extraordinary courage. Most of those who acted against the Nazi-Fascists were common folk holding to moral values alien to war and oppression.

This, therefore, requires a reassessment of the period. There should be recognition that the material, psychological, idealistic and spiritual acts of opposition to the Nazi occupation and fascism, expressed in a non-violent way, should no longer be implied or considered as mere support to the armed partisan struggle.

This book shines a light on extraordinary doings by unknown heroes, in the hope that historians will continue the search for such forms of resistance. The facts must be made evident, to give credit to the thousands of men and women who built the new Italy: people who should not be confused with those who did what suited them and who were probably the very same who filled the squares during the fascist rallies. There is no need to judge the latter because, in their servile way, such people will be ever-present in history. What is important instead is to study the behaviour of all those who, while not participating in the partisan struggle, helped bring down the dictatorship.

There were, then, two kinds of resistance: the armed, partisan Resistance, which was certainly politicised and which began to split along party lines within the CLN; and the unarmed resistance, which was unknowingly politicised but was outside party structures. The reason that unarmed resisters have escaped a census is that they were not included within co-ordinated resistance groups.

Unarmed resistance was manifest in the following ways:

□ Boycotts: tacit disobedience to the laws of state, creating logistical problems for the authorities.

☐ Draft dodging: the refusal by those born in 1923, 1924 and 1925 to answer the call to arms and be drafted into the new army of the Republic of Salò.

☐ Sabotage: the destruction of posters, road signs and agricultural machinery, impeding the circulation of military columns and preventing the expropriation of agricultural products.

☐ Strikes in protest at the German occupation and in favour of peace.

☐ Popular demonstrations demanding the release of men who had been rounded up.

☐ Circulation of a clandestine press.

☐ Assistance for those on the run: shelter and food for Jews, draft dodgers and especially former Allied prisoners.

Only in recent years has Italian historiography paid closer attention to the forms of unarmed resistance deployed during the war. Leading historians of the Resistance, starting with Roberto Battaglia and Giorgio Bocca, addressed the issue in purely military terms, reconstructing almost exclusively the partisan war. Liberation from Nazi-Fascism was thus seen as the result of armed confrontation. The historian Renzo De Felice was another who supported a military thesis, maintaining that a civil war broke out in Italy after 8 September 1943 featuring two opposing minorities: on one side about 200,000 partisans and on the other approximately 500,000 soldiers of the Italian Social Republic.

Viewed in this way, if one includes the family members of both sides, at most there were about four million Italians involved in the conflict. The rest of the population, totalling about 44 million, constituted a grey area, which, according to De Felice, was indifferent to the military and political outcome.[4]

It was quite otherwise. Because of the civil resistance, the liberation from Nazi-Fascism was a mass experience and one of democratic participation. Therefore, the historian Anna Bravo maintains, we should move on from "the idea of implicit unfairness regarding the positions that continue to identify partisan resistance and civil resistance, when it is rather of armed resistance that we should talk about, leaving the noun 'resistance' open to other meanings. It is not formalism. Without erasing the distinctions, an adjective would give to each his own right: to the fighters the coat of arms, not the monopoly of the fight and the foundation of democracy; to those who have shared the status of defender in different forms it should not be by promotion, but by right."[5]

The civil resistance also enables us to comprehend the gap that existed between the fascist regime and society during the war years. Men and women felt the need to choose freedom by courageously committing themselves and running enormous risks. In some cases the military authorities themselves disregarded orders emanating from the fascist government or the Germans.

A little-known episode is the dissent of General de Castiglioni and his so-called "soft occupation" of the region of Isère, in the south of France. Despite pressure from the Italian and German governments he decided not to proceed with the arrest and deportation of Jews, while also impeding repressive operations by the Vichy government.[6] The stance taken by de Castiglioni and many other Italian commanders even compelled [Adolf] Eichmann, the "accountant of extermination", to complain to Mussolini. The Duce apologised, citing as explanation "the different intellectual make-up" of some Italians.

According to the historian Hannah Arendt, "Italy was one of the few countries in Europe where every anti-Semitic measure was decisively unpopular. This was because, in the words of [Gian Galeazzo] Ciano [foreign minister and son-in-law of Mussolini], the measures 'created problems that didn't exist'. The assimilation (to use this much abused word) of Jews was a reality in Italy."[7]

A complex aspect of the resistance was the role of the Italian military internees, the soldiers deported to Germany. Only recently has their reputation been restored after years of defamatory judgments that condemned them as indolent and social outcasts. In the eyes of many, they were outcasts. Even left-wing parties shared this prejudice. An account in the 1960s by Alessandro Natta, a post-war Communist Party leader, in which he recorded his memories and political opinions with regard to his military imprisonment, met with rejection. In his book, which was only published in 1997 under the title *The Other Resistance*, he maintained: "Because of its origin and nature, it is generally agreed both by the Italians who suffered the punishment and the Germans who inflicted it, that it was an episode of political struggle rather than a military one."[8]

Another important form of unarmed resistance that took place in Italy was the strike. The first strikes to materialise were in Turin in March 1943. However, their political character became more evident when, on 1 March 1944, in the face of full Nazi-Fascist occupation, all work stopped almost simultaneously in factories in the north, at the behest of the CLN. Turin and Milan were at

Filippo Ieranò

the centre of this action. The strike lasted eight days and
was a model of co-operation between workers, students
and partisans.

Threats made by General [Bodo] Zimmermann were
worthless and only on 8 March, on the order of the strike
committee, did the workers return. The strike mobilised
1.2 million workers and was recognised as ". . . the most
important ever in invaded Europe".[9]

Le Marche, given the low presence of industrial sites,
remained on the fringes of worker protests. But the
reception given by the civilian population to the people
on the wanted list (Jews, partisans and escaped Allied
prisoners) meant the region was actively involved in the
struggle.

After its initial victories from 1941 to 1942, Italy found
itself holding thousands of Allied prisoners, often
interned in buildings that had been used during the First
World War. It is estimated that in September 1943 there
were 80,000 Allied prisoners present in camps dotted
across the centre and north of the peninsular. There were
three camps in Le Marche: Sforzacosta, near Macerata;
Fermo, in the commune of Campiglione; and Servigliano.
The last two camps were located in the Tenna Valley.

The escape of hundreds of prisoners, the proximity to
the Front and the presence of many Jewish families in
internment transformed this pleasant area into one of
confrontation, in which simple, ordinary people turned
into silent heroes and unknown protagonists showed
great humanity and civic courage. Above all, it is through
them that the popular character of the resistance
becomes evident. In the Fermano it is believed that
several thousand people on the wanted list, perhaps
10,000, were helped and saved from the Germans. Taking

into account the close relationships between families, friends and neighbours, one can conclude that the overwhelming majority of the 140,000 inhabitants of the Tenna Valley were involved in rescuing those on the run.

This display of moral strength has won the admiration of contemporary historians such as English historian Roger Absalom, who writes of the "great alliance" between the *contadini* and the prisoners. Absalom believes that this solidarity found its root in the Christian tradition. The historian Anna Bravo disagrees and concludes, after a close study of the civil resistance, that the reception of those on the run had a psychological character, one showing maternal aspects.

They are both interesting interpretations but they do not explain why neither religious fervour nor maternal instinct made itself apparent in May 1942 when a dozen Allied soldiers fled from Servigliano camp and were recaptured within a few days in the absence of rescue by the people. It is always difficult to interpret events this complex. In any case, the "Other Resistance" must be reconsidered as having civic and political importance.

"He who protects a persecuted person does not wait, he does not make salvation of the person secondary to the victorious end of war, which might come further down the road. He makes his choice and shows his hand and through his behaviour he exemplifies the simple and crucial relationship that exists between the theme of civil resistance and that of personal responsibility," as one historian commented.[10]

At Servigliano in the Tenna Valley, and throughout Le Marche and the rest of Italy occupied by the Nazi-Fascists, people simply went two different ways after the Armistice of 8 September 1943, expressing radically

27

different choices. On the one hand, the hard and convinced core of fascism reconstituted itself, adhering fully to the logic of "absolute evil" pursued by Nazism. On the other hand, the vast majority of the people chose freedom, expressed in recognising the fundamental human rights of those on the wanted list. The principles underlying those experiences would later become enshrined as articles of the Italian Constitution that came into force in January 1948.

Assistance afforded to those on the run was something that was particularly feared by the Nazi-Fascists, so much so that Mussolini threatened terrible reprisals against transgressors. "Anyone who in any way helps prisoners fleeing from the concentration camps, or gives hospitality to members of the enemy's armed forces with the intention of enabling their flight or concealing their presence, will face the death penalty."[11]

All those who showed generosity to Allied prisoners did so at enormous risk. They did so voluntarily! But along with the threats came promises of substantial recompense to those who co-operated with authorities, bearing in mind that 2,000 lira was the equivalent of about three months' wages for a worker. There was double that sum if it were a Jew who was denounced. To encourage collaboration, the authorities also proposed the exchange of personnel: anybody who denounced an Allied prisoner might be able to recover a relative interned in one of the Reich's camps. It meant a tough choice for unarmed people. Some paid for their generosity with their lives.

For confirmation of the special nature of the Italian civil resistance it is worth looking at events at Mauthausen concentration camp. From spring 1944 there were plans to exterminate the mainly Soviet prisoners interned at this camp in north Austria, an integral part of the Third Reich. The project – codenamed Operation K, from *kugel* (bullet) – had already led to the deaths of more than 4,400 prisoners by the start of 1945 and a prisoner arriving at the camp soon became aware that he was in store for a miserable death.

On 2 February 1945 about 500 Russian prisoners managed to escape, many seeking salvation by heading for Czechoslovakia, where there was a resistance network. As soon as the escape was discovered the SS commander put into action Operation "Hunt the Hares", involving civilians above all. In the snow-covered countryside, with sub-zero temperatures, hundreds of armed men with scores of vehicles gave chase to the fugitives. The population, perhaps influenced by Nazi propaganda that incited hatred of Russians, enthusiastically participated in the "hunting party". The captured prisoners were summarily shot and their bodies stacked in macabre heaps.

A tragic toll, but not all the 500 fugitives were eliminated. Seventeen succeeded in saving themselves; just a very few, but evidence that not all Germans were "Hitler's volunteer executioners".[12] Some families chose to help the fleeing prisoners, saving their lives.

This episode was similar in many ways to those that occurred in the Tenna Valley. But while the Italian families were part of a mass resistance, those few families around Mauthausen who hid Russian prisoners did so under conditions of greater danger and solitude. The involvement of civilians, their participation in the round-ups and the willing use of arms against fleeing Russian prisoners worn down by months of hunger and maltreatment is baffling. And yet, for more than four months, some families hid 17 wanted men until the arrival of liberating forces, when the survivors returned to their own regiments.

The 20th century had already witnessed acts of spontaneous or organised disobedience, such as Mahatma Gandhi's struggle against the British in India. "Civil disobedience is the citizen's intrinsic right. He dare not give it up without ceasing to be a man," said the Mahatma. For Gandhi, civil disobedience was a tactic of political struggle that went hand in hand with spiritual growth. The denial of violence should extend both to one's social commitment and to one's personal behaviour. Non-violence presents choices that involve one personally in campaigns of mass disobedience, boycotts and resistance to tyrannical power.

In the same years in which this new model of political fight was being formulated in India, Tolstoy – who was in contact with Gandhi and was aware of H. Thoreau's essay "Civil disobedience" – came up with his principle of "non-resistance to evil with violence", citing also Jesus's Sermon on the Mount.

In Italy, while spontaneous forms of unarmed civil resistance were materialising, Aldo Capitini, a theorist of non-violence, was suffering imprisonment for his ideas. He, like other unarmed resisters, was to become marginalised in the reporting of the Resistance by historians of the second half of the 20th century. Even today Capitini, founder of the Nonviolence Movement and organiser of the Perugia to Assisi March for Peace, is unknown to most.

It was he who coined the word "nonviolence" without the hyphen to underline that it should not be interpreted as a negation of violence but rather as a term rich in its own meaning.

In addition to the theorising in opposition to violence and the dismantling of ideologies that preached genocide, people were proposing the vanquishing of brutality with love, overturning the Machiavellian and western logic of "the end justifies the means". From "If you want peace, prepare for war"[13] the cry became "If you want peace, prepare for peace".[14]

Evidently ideas are borne on the wind, considering what happened in the Tenna Valley – where it was neither a hero nor a prophet, but an entire people, who put themselves out to help thousands of wanted persons without regard to racial or religious differences. Gandhi had the intuition to interpret similar actions of solidarity and to recognise in them the force of justice that springs from man's conscience. History, therefore, becomes not only the relating of violent events, battles, victories and defeats, and of kings and dictators, but the story of people.

The contribution and writings of Don Lorenzo Milani [an educator of poor children and an advocate of conscientious objection] are particularly relevant. In the 1960s, profiting from his own experience as a teacher, he wrote: "I had to make it very clear in my teaching how the citizen reacts to injustice. How he benefits from free speech and freedom of the press. How the Christian resists a priest who errs, even a bishop. How everyone must feel himself responsible for everything. On a wall of our classroom is written in capitals 'I CARE'. It is the untranslatable motto of the best young Americans. 'It matters to me, it is close to my heart.' It is the exact opposite of the fascist motto 'I don't care a jot'."[15]

The words recognise the right to civil disobedience as a building block of democratic societies. The protagonists of the events reported in this volume were witnesses to this revolution in ideals. In the face of oppressive legislation they adhered to greater values, ones nurtured by the conscience. These men and women put into practice principles that were to be at the heart of the Italian Constitution.

1. Mario Rotta, order of 26 July 1943 for maintaining public order.

2. http:www.istoreco.re.it

3. Renzo De Felice, preface in Elena Aga Rossi, *L'inganno reciproco*, the Armistice between Italy and the Anglo-Americans of September 1943, Ministero per I Beni Culturali e Ambientali – Ufficio Centrali per I beni archivistici, Rome 1993.

4. Renzo De Felice, *Breve storia del fascismo*, Oscar Mondadori, Milan 2004, p. 123.

5. Edited by Anna Bravo and Daniele Jallà, *Una misura onesta*, FrancoAngeli, Milan 1994, p. 3.

6. Various authors, *L'Isère en resistance*, Grenoble, Le dauphine, 2005, pp. 40–41.

7. H. Arendt, *La banalità del male*, Feltrinelli, Milan 2003, p. 183.

8. Alessandro Natta, *L'altra Resistenza*, Giulio Einaudi Editore, Turin 1997, p. 5.

9. R. Battaglia and G. Garritano, *Breve storia della Resistenza Italiana*, Editori Riubniti, Rome 1976, p. 70.

10. Various authors, *Le radici della Resistenza – Donne e guerra, donne in guerra*, Rome Pisa, Edizioni Plus, 2005, p. 49.

11. B. Mussolini, Decree of 9/10/1943, Art 1.

12. Daniel Goldagen, *I volonterosi carnefici di Hitler*, Mondadori, Milan 1996. According to the author, the German people not only knew of the extermination policy pursued by Nazism but openly supported it.

13. From the Latin Si vis pacem para bellum.

14. An overturning of the preceding Latin phrase, used by pacifists in the second half of the 19th century.

15. Don Lorenzo Milani, *L'obbedienza non è piu una virtù*, Florence 1965.

The setting

Servigliano camp

In 1915, when Italy entered the First World War, work began at Servigliano to build a large internment camp for Austro–Hungarian prisoners. After the expropriation of approximately 30,000 square metres of land, about 40 wooden and brick barracks were constructed, each of 500 square metres. In addition, several brick huts were put up outside the surrounding walls to house the guards. The camp was situated on the village border, near the station that served the railway running through the Tenna Valley from Porto San Giorgio to Amandola. In total the camp could hold nearly 4,000 inmates. In 1918, at the end of the war, the Austro–Hungarian prisoners were repatriated. The following year the site was put to use as a re-education camp for "redeemed" Italian soldiers [prisoners from Istria, Dalmatia and Trentino, who, as subjects of the Habsburg Empire, had fought in the Austro–Hungarian army].

In 1920 the camp was closed for prisoners and adapted to hold military supplies, and in 1935 the fascist regime conceded half of it to the Community After-Work programme in order to create a football pitch, which is still in operation.

In 1941, when Italy entered the Second World War alongside the Germans, the camp was reorganised to hold Allied prisoners of war of various nationalities: Greek, Maltese, Cypriot, British, American, French and Slav.

A few days after the announcement of the Armistice on 8 September 1943 about 200 prisoners escaped, pouring out into the Tenna Valley to be welcomed by ordinary people, in particular the *contadini*. On the arrival of the Germans and the return of the fascists, the site was transformed into an internment camp for Jews and civilians. Scores of internees were transferred from Servigliano to Fossoli camp [in Emilia Romagna] and thence to extermination camps in Germany.

In June 1944 the Germans completed their retreat from the Tenna Valley. On arrival, the Allies immediately closed the camp and repatriated the internees. It was then used, however, as a training camp for about 1,000 Polish soldiers and the following year was transformed into a refugee centre. The first arrivals were Slovenian but, from 1947 onwards, it accepted only Italian refugees from the Julian March and Dalmatian areas [re-assigned to Yugoslavia]. In 1955 the site was closed and abandoned until the 1970s, when it became a public park. Since 2001 the Casa della Memoria association has worked to turn it into a memorial site.

The themes

This chapter discusses the most important themes arising out of the various narratives set out in Part Three.

The prisoners

Today, next to the town of Servigliano, there are new houses that encircle the beautiful and historic 18th century centre. However, in 1915, when the prison camp was constructed to hold Austro–Hungarian PoWs, a strip of countryside separated the town from the camp. The authorities intended to keep the two separate in order to avoid any sort of relationship between the Italians and their enemies, imprisoned on the other side of the high boundary wall. Still, there was no lack of opportunities for contact between prisoners and populace, especially among those prisoners who were engaged in farm work with the local peasants.

This type of contact occurred again, and much more extensively, during the Second World War. Servigliano camp was reopened to accommodate "enemy prisoners" in 1941, two years after the outbreak of the war. Except that this time fascist Italy had the Third Reich as an ally, including Germany and Austria, while the western democracies, including the British and Americans – the Allies – were now the enemy. At the beginning of 1941 the first prisoners to arrive were Greek, who were then transferred on to other camps. In 1942 British and other Commonwealth nationalities arrived, to be replaced in 1943 by American prisoners.

A black market, tolerated by the authorities, spontaneously arose between the camp guards and the prisoners, and also with the civilians on the outside. Food items contained in the prisoners' Red Cross parcels were exchanged for local foodstuffs and other general articles. Cigarettes were the most sought-after commodity.

Renzo Zocchi says that everyone was aware of the presence of prisoners of war, but not of their identity. He was able to approach some prisoners thanks to an uncle who owned a small plot of land, close to the high wall surrounding the camp, where there was a large cherry tree.

". . . when the fruit was ripe, I could throw cherries over the wall towards the prisoners." (see Renzo Zocchi)

Of course, care had to be taken either that the guards, other than those who were also in on the scheme, were not around or could be distracted. There was no lack of gratitude in return.

"The prisoners, to thank me, threw me some bars of soap. That was probably stuff that they had received in their Red Cross parcels." (Renzo Zocchi)

Although the constant movement of the prisoners prevented any real knowledge of their identity, rumours leaked out.

". . . when picking the cherries, I often saw prisoners but never the same faces. It was difficult for me to know what nationality they were; I only knew that they were prisoners of war. In the village, people said there were Jewish people, Americans . . . but these were only rumours." (Renzo Zocchi)

The guards were also a source of information and of exchange between villagers and the prison camp. The best meeting places were the bars and wine shops. There, between a drink and a game of cards, things were revealed.

". . . [the people of Servigliano's] only involvement was with the guards who spent money in the local shops and attended the bars in the evening." (Renzo Zocchi)

Enrico Marziali tells of his brother who, despite having the job of camp cook, was unable to provide any detailed news.

"We knew little about the camp. Vincenzo was a cook, not a guard, and he didn't have contact with prisoners. We knew somehow that there were lots of prisoners and that they were guarded by the soldiers." (Enrico Marziali)

The eighth of September

On 8 September 1943, when the news spread of the signing of the Armistice between Italy and the Allies, the reaction was one of joy and exultation, in the belief that, at least as far as Italy was concerned, the war was over. Perhaps it was hoped that this could exorcise the danger that Germany now represented, as an abandoned ally betrayed in the midst of the war. The radio continuously replayed the news, and the reaction of the ordinary people is easy to imagine:

"As soon as the news of the Armistice got out there was an explosion of joy because we were convinced that the war would be over." (see Licinio Licini)

"I was about 22 when the news of the Armistice got out. Everyone welcomed it with enthusiasm, saying: 'The war is over! The war is over!'" (Amelia Antodicola)

"At home we were happy and thought it would mean no more shooting. . . . We were all convinced that the war was over." (Renzo Zocchi)

Many believed, or at least hoped, that the nightmare was really over. Divisions between the Supreme Command close to the king and the military units stationed far from the headquarters in Rome meant extreme tension for the Italian armed forces. The military hierarchy collapsed, leaving ordinary soldiers to make serious decisions for themselves: should they continue to fight? Alongside the Germans or the Allies?

"On 8 September 1943 I was in Rome, at Tiburtina. The king had run away with Badoglio and we were abandoned! I was in the air force and was part of a detachment of the Third Air Squadron, near Tiburtina station. The news of the Armistice was announced in the evening, around five o'clock, or maybe seven or eight, I don't remember exactly. That day I went to see my uncle, Giovanni, a colonel who worked in the War Department. We all thought with relief that the war was over and when I returned to the barracks we were absolutely euphoric. But a day later, on 9 September, there were no clear instructions, the officers did not know what to do and they

were continuously ringing the switchboard of the Air Ministry, where no-one answered. There was an increasing sense of anxiety amongst us soldiers, and it was impossible to fully understand the situation." (Neno Brugnolini)

"I remember that on 8 September there was a serious stampede . . ." (Giovanni Pilotti)

"From the first days after the Armistice our army's disbanded soldiers began to pass by. They wandered around like poor stray dogs. They were scared, suspicious, hungry and in miserable tattered clothing. My father had a piece of bread for everyone and gladly added a word of comfort." (Abramo Marzialetti)

Meanwhile, at home, the joyful news prompted an anxious wait.

"In a few days many of those who had been called up returned; they arrived on foot, tired and dirty, passing through the fields to get home as soon as possible. And when the news spread of someone's return there were kisses and tears, even the church bell rang in celebration." (Diva Papiri)

"When we heard about the Armistice on 8 September I got cracking and gave permission to the soldiers on duty in the fortress of Viterbo to leave and return to their homes." (Luciano Iommi)

Those waiting were also concerned about the Italian prisoners who were in the hands of the Allies. Several hundred thousand men were spread around hundreds of camps established across the vast British Empire, from India to Australia, from South Africa to Scotland.

"At home we were all happy and our thoughts turned to a cousin, a prisoner in Africa, who it was hoped would return soon." (Licinio Licini)

Instead, those expectations were disappointed. The Germans crossed the Brenner Pass with thousands of well-armed men and occupied the centre and north of Italy, imposing on Mussolini a new government and a new state, the Italian Social Republic, whose only task was to repress partisan forces and all forms of anti-fascism.

In a few days Italy, the "Bel Paese", entered a new phase, becoming the theatre for both political and military confrontations. For the Jews it was the beginning of a new tragedy.

". . . one October morning four Carabinieri turned up and surrounded the house, announcing that we were under arrest. They took us to their headquarters at Porto San Giorgio. Here they allotted a number to each of us. If I remember correctly, my father got the number 16, my mother 17, my brother 18 and I got 19. We stayed there for a few hours with the other Jews who had been arrested; they were mostly former internees. Then they handed us over to the Germans who took us by truck to Servigliano." (Carla Viterbo)

The great escape

The Armistice brought turmoil, not only to the Italian civilians and their military but also to the prisoners in the camps, including Servigliano, who gave themselves over to displays of exultation.

But, as the hours went by, fear began to spread among those hundreds of men.

Although, after the announcement of the Armistice, many were convinced that the Allied front at Pescara would quickly reach the southern Marche and liberate Servigliano, a couple of days later the disappointment was palpable and a bitter nervousness crept in, mainly due to the news of Germany's invasion of Italy. The indecision of the camp commandants contributed to a rising tension, with the men feeling themselves still prisoners, under the guns of the armed guards who remained in place in the watchtowers.

The news that circulated from hour to hour was that the Germans were getting closer and closer to Servigliano. It seemed a mockery that they should all be found in the camp like rats in a trap, waiting for the Italian guards to be replaced by Teutonic ones. Worryingly, some Italian guards had already vanished. Another reason for uncertainty was due to the orders of the Allied command, which didn't hide its distrust of both the government of Badoglio and of the Italians in general. For this reason, and despite the rapid German advance along the peninsula, British authorities gave the order that the Allied prisoners should not leave the camps, to avoid a one-sided confrontation between unarmed prisoners and well-armed and trained German troops. There was also the risk that civilians would come into conflict with the

Allied prisoners on the run, as they had been enemies until a few days earlier.

In this climate the prisoners of the Servigliano camp called an assembly to decide what to do. Captain John Millar, an English medical officer, spoke to the crowd of prisoners who were quite clear that they could not accept the fate of surrendering without resistance to the Germans.

The assembly voted for the escape and the camp disgorged 2,000 men, who poured out into an unknown countryside, filled with people with whom they had had no prior contact. For everyone, escape meant heading south, towards Pescara. The territory was inhabited by hardworking peasants who immediately noticed their presence.

"Since the Armistice there had been news of the prisoners escaping, rumours circulated that the guards had opened the gates of the prison camps of Servigliano and of Monte Urano. It was known that in the woods around Montefalcone there were several of them, but I hadn't ever seen any." (see Diva Papiri)

For many locals the prisoners' arrival among them was an unforeseen novelty, and brought with it tension, fear or simply emotion.

"I don't remember exactly when the prisoners escaped, perhaps a day or two after the initial confusion, but it definitely happened at night. There were lots of them, so many it was like a carnival, all running away. A few hundred metres away from the camp there was a bank with thick scrub, acacias all full of thorns, considered

43

impenetrable, but the prisoners threw themselves in there in heaps, like a landslide, flattening it, and this all while the guards were shooting." (Gino Leoni)

Not many mention these shots and, perhaps, the whole truth will never be known. According to Sandro Kanzaghi, a Greek prisoner fell in this scrub, badly wounded by a shot fired by an Italian camp guard. He lay in agony all night, screaming and asking in vain for help. By the first light of dawn, when a Carabinieri patrol moved in to look for him, his screams had stopped. After a while, in the thick of the undergrowth, the soldiers found the lifeless body of the prisoner.

"The fascists were certainly firing. A Greek from Cyprus screamed in agony all night, and only the day after was he taken to the cemetery." (Gino Leoni)

"They were walking in small groups, here and there, doing their best to keep a low profile. That will have been the 9th or 10th of September. . . . Others made up improvised tents, hidden in the gully, and stayed there for a few days." (Renzo Zocchi)

The peasants came to recognise the many different nationalities of the prisoners, including the eastern Allies.

"When the camp at Servigliano was opened up, all the prisoners left: there were Americans, English, Slavs, Russians, a bit of everything. At first they went around the houses with a certain ease and many of them came to Montelparo. Only a few came to the village, though; most

asked for refuge in the countryside instead." (Amelia Antodicola)

Initial contact was driven by the prisoners' basic need for shelter and of hunger. The prisoners would knock on doors or otherwise cautiously approach a farmhouse. And there, inside those simple houses, the peasants responded as they had always done, respecting a universal ethic that belongs to the rural world across all continents: welcoming foreigners in difficulty. Those well-worn doors, which barely held out the icy breath of the north wind, opened to take in unknown men speaking an unknown language, but obviously in need.

"Our parents understood the misery of the prisoners on the run, some of them had also been in the First War and knew what hunger meant or the discomfort of sleeping under the stars, in the cold. I remember my parents gave us loaves of bread, about a kilo, baked in the wood oven, to take to the prisoners hidden in the gully. . . . We were never short of bread; in the country it was the one thing we always had plenty of." (Renzo Zocchi)

"When the first prisoners appeared, my Mum was on a piece of land that we had on the Tennacola and she immediately realised who they were." (Giovanni Pilotti)

As the days passed, the rescues turned from a spontaneous and private gesture to one organised collectively through a network based on friendship, family and neighbourliness.

Filippo Ieranò

"We lived in the centre of the village and the people there also mobilised to rescue the prisoners. So Dad and Mum said we could take one too. That was how we got to know Robert." (Amelia Antodicola)

Every time, and in every place, after every first meeting, identities were revealed and relationships were built. The strangers had a name and prejudices fell away. Now the peasants recognised in the fleeing prisoners merely other men who were in need.

"I remember that a Slav came to my house. His name was Novak, a name that has stayed with me. . . . He was good, a really good man!" (Lino Luciani)

Meanwhile there was a growing expectation among the families that their own relatives, Italian prisoners in the hands of the Allies, would soon return.

"After the news of the Armistice in 1943 everyone was happy and my dear Mum said: 'Now my boys will come home.' She was thinking of Florindo, who was a prisoner in Greece, and Alberigo, who was in Africa." (Arduina Rossi)

After the great escape of 14 September 1943 the site was used as an internment camp for Jews. There were only a few dozen people, who were rounded up in the province of Ascoli. Yet, despite the small number, there were other escapes. In particular, that of 4 May 1944 is remembered because it involved all the inmates, about 60 Jews. All dispersed along the Tenna scrub, but only 29 managed to find help from the locals. The other 31 returned the next morning to the town square, unaware of the fate that awaited them. Behind the slits in the blinds, many eyes watched what happened: some German vehicles arrived and picked up the Jews present, one by one, to transfer them to the camp at Fossoli[1] and from there, by train, to the Auschwitz concentration camp. These were the last acts of the Nazi-Fascist occupation in the Tenna Valley. The Allied land troops, almost exclusively Polish units, advanced along the Adriatic coast. Alongside them was the CIL (Italian Liberation Corps)[2], which operated only as auxiliary support. Meanwhile the opposition to the Nazi-Fascists was carried out by ordinary people and by partisan formations. In fact this popular mobilisation took on the characteristics of an unarmed struggle which, today, is defined as civil resistance.

Despite the fact that nine months had passed since the beginning of the German occupation, Carla Viterbo, one of the 29 Jews aided and sheltered by forgotten heroes, confirms that in those days of May 1944 the unarmed resistance was still able to cope with the latest emergency.

"My father knew a local doctor. . . . It was this doctor who welcomed us into his house the following morning." (Carla Viterbo)

Asking for help

In the days following the great escape of 14 September 1943 weather conditions worsened quickly, bringing in winter temperatures. The first snow appeared early on the Sibillini mountains and the condition of the Allied prisoners became critical. The various makeshift shelters, caves, abandoned barns and dilapidated houses could not guarantee even minimal comfort. It was not the desire for human contact but the urgent necessity to satisfy one's basic needs that prompted former prisoners to ask for help.

". . . as the weather worsened, they began to approach the houses to ask for shelter. Not just in our home, also others in the area, spreading themselves out among different families." (see Renzo Zocchi)

Hunger was added to the hardship of the cold, since everyone's supplies, taken from the camp warehouse or Red Cross parcels, were quickly exhausted, making their days more and more unbearable.

"At the beginning there were at least five prisoners at our house: they were English, American and one was Jewish. . . . It was hunger that brought them to us." (Renzo Zocchi)

"Bring him, whoever he is! One more mouth to feed won't matter!" (Enrico Marziali)

Those who welcomed the men were able see in their pale faces the hardships which the former prisoners had suffered by deciding to flee.

"However, it was impossible to refuse a bit of bread to somebody in those circumstances." (Enrico Marziali)

"Dad asked them: 'How long have you been here?' 'For days, for days. We hungry, we are hungry,' they answered." (Diva Papiri)

These were difficult times for everyone and the food shortage was also felt in the farmhouses. Still, the peasants showed solidarity and a spirit of sharing that was heroic. They understood that only their help could save the hunted men.

". . . [the prisoners] lived off whatever the peasants could offer, who helped them with great selflessness." (Giovanni Pilotti)

The danger

The great escape from the camp occurred on 14 September and the arrival of the Germans in Servigliano is recorded as occurring on the evening of the 15th, just 24 hours later. But, while the former Allied prisoners went into hiding in the scrub and gullies, the German troops organised a system of control over the territory, starting with the occupation of the main centres. Republican fascism certainly played a fundamental role in this plan, a role required by Hitler but with Mussolini at its head. After the humiliation of 25 July [when Mussolini had been deposed and his supporters were forced to lie low], veteran fascists now collaborated wholeheartedly with the Germans, planning revenge against their political opponents.

"The greater danger, however, came from the fascists who, alarmed by the American advance, often used the

Germans for personal vendettas." (see Amelia Antodicola)

The army of Salò[3] had new followers, though in truth not that many, just those who were young and receptive to the fascist propaganda that trumpeted the value of honour and fidelity to their German ally. They were all set up as local government officials, subject to German control. But, among those called to arms, most went into hiding.[4]

"I too had to go into hiding, because Mussolini had recalled everyone to arms, but I did not appear." (Neno Brugnolini)

In the second half of September the Germans decided to use the Servigliano camp for the internment of Jews living in the province of Ascoli. Military pressure and the climate of fear that the Nazi-Fascists tried to establish had a clear purpose: to eliminate all forms of resistance and obtain the absolute respect of the rules imposed by the German military command. In line with this strategy, the soldiers did not hesitate to shoot at unarmed civilians. More often than not those shots were aimed at the backs of defenceless people. Even Servigliano suffered a massacre, near the camp, with husband and wife Nicola and Marina Viozzi the victims.[5] There was widespread fear.

". . . we were always afraid of the Germans." (Renzo Zocchi)

"All of us, everyone was in fear. It wasn't just for one or two of us, it was everyone." (Lino Luciani)

"The fear was such that not even our three dogs barked." (Cesare Viozzi)

But when groups of German soldiers, flanked by soldiers of the neo-fascist government of Salò, began to roam the countryside, contact between peasants and ex-prisoners had already taken place and affection had grown. An implicit pact of freedom had been formed. When the armoured cars suddenly swooped into farmyards, they found the peasants busy in their stables, manure piles and woodsheds, with the prisoners already safely hidden.

"One day [the Germans] turned up without us having seen them coming." (Renzo Zocchi)

"The Germans did come by to search the house, luckily just a few days after the prisoners had left." (Gino Leoni)

"Of course, we were worried, also because we heard of some family who, having given aid to the prisoners, had suffered violence from the Germans and fascists. But we were very careful." (Licinio Licini)

As the days and weeks went by there came into being, in addition to the various forms of non-violent civil resistance that spontaneously arose in the countryside and small villages, the partisan Resistance that provided military opposition to the occupying forces.

Filippo Ieranò

"There were very hard days during which the partisan gang which I commanded was continually attacked by fascists and Germans." (Manuel Serrano)

From November 1943 the Germans initiated a widespread strategy of terror, most effectively using surprise searches. They would arrive in strength out of the blue and forcefully surround a house, throwing everyone into a panic.

"Immediately some soldiers jumped down and one of them took my mother by the arm and said confidently, in broken Italian: 'Mother, you have an Englishman in this house named Billy!'" (Licinio Licini)

"Around then we heard of a round-up by the Nazi-Fascists and the capture of some English prisoners and of young Italian draft dodgers, who all ended up in camps in Germany. Seriously, the fear of being discovered was so strong." (Renato Corradini)

The fear was so great because there was scarcely a house that was not somehow involved in rescuing wanted men. And the news of disproportionate violence against defenceless people was spreading from valley to valley.

". . . some families had their houses burned down for giving aid to prisoners, nearby, along the river Ete." (Neno Brugnolini)

"So they beat him up – who knows how many blows they gave him – until they let him go, bruised all over. But he

hadn't told, he didn't say where the prisoners were hidden." (Diva Papiri)

". . . an Englishman, David, an intellectual. I saw him shot outside the village." (Amelia Antodicola)

"The danger persisted and became more and more pressing. The Germans and the fascists, angry at the events that were occurring, became really determined. They raided our house several times and once it was really nasty. That time, unusually, we were taken by surprise and found them already there." (Abramo Marzialetti)

". . . I learned that there had been round-ups and that, during one of these, a Republican[6] had shot an Englishman. The prisoner died almost immediately from his injuries at the hospital in Penna and was buried in the town cemetery." (Giovanni Pilotti)

"Before leaving they fired bursts of machine gun fire at the walls of the house and maybe even threw hand grenades at the windows, terrorising everyone and shattering the glass. Another soldier came and, seeing that we had a horse, ordered us to hand it over. The retreating Germans took everything!" (Cesare Viozzi)

There was certainly no lack of imaginative methods used to save the ex-prisoners. Someone even came up with a kind of disguise.

"In the evening, to get Billy to this lady in the village, my mother resorted to a disguise: she made him dress as a woman, using her aunt's clothes. At that time there was

no-one around in the streets anyway, and with a handkerchief around his head he was unrecognisable. They went out together, Billy and Mum, like two ladies, and they managed to reach the house of grandmother's maid without any problem." (Licinio Licini)

The welcome

Yet, despite the risks, the people of the Tenna Valley were not overcome by their fear. Almost all of them ignored the menacing proclamations posted on the walls of the village houses and at crossroads, even on the remote farmhouses lost in the folds of the countryside. Their reaction to this fear was not a complex intellectual exercise, much less the result of a thoughtful and conscious political choice. No! The families opened their doors to those wanted by the Nazi-Fascists from an inner sense of goodness. Being faced with the difficulties of the prisoners on the run generated strong feelings of brotherly or filial love. And that welcome, inevitably, also led to one conscious choice, which was a profound rejection of war.

". . . at home there were lots of anti-war sentiments expressed and people were persuaded that it was right to help the prisoners on the run. Not that we thought too much about the risks: we couldn't but help them, poor things!" (see Renzo Zocchi*)*

"We looked after him at home because he was in a really awful state." (Superio Marinangeli)

". . . I invited them to come to our house where we could find something to meet their needs." (Renato Corradini)

"Dad came into the house bringing this boy with him . . ." (Amelia Antodicola)

"They asked if we had any room for them." (Arduina Rossi)

The welcome extended to the fleeing Allied prisoners was linked to the sad condition of their own relatives, prisoners of the Allies, in places unimaginably distant. Thus the feelings of affection and nostalgia for loved ones far away nourished and confirmed the gestures of help towards these other prisoners, in the hope of an unlikely reciprocity.

". . . when she saw them my poor mother immediately thought of my brothers, prisoners of the British and the Americans, and from whom we had had no news." (Gino Leoni)

Added to the heroic welcome was a duty to provide comfort and psychological support. These were people beset by difficulties, lost in unknown territory and sheltered by people they considered enemies. Sometimes the tension was such as to lead to despair. That was the case for Carla Viterbo and her family, who escaped from Servigliano camp, where they were interned as Jews, and found shelter with the Franciscans of Fermo. There her father had an emotional breakdown. Escape, hiding, fear of violent repercussions had led him to decide to give himself up. He was in despair.

It was a difficult situation. It was also madness, because this gesture would have dragged the whole family into the abyss. Luckily Father Galli intervened to support him and make him reflect, to appease the inner turmoil of an honest person hunted like a common thug.

"In those moments I saw the tensions between two people of different religions: the desperation of my father and the courage of Father Galli." (Carla Viterbo)

The families

The world of the *contadino* in the 1940s was a patriarchal one, a historic model given a boost by fascist politics. Patriarchal families, made up of several nuclear families united by a strong blood bond, lived in large houses built both of bricks fashioned out of the abundant local clay and of stones extracted from the fields. Typically the ground floor was intended for the kitchen and work (stable, wine-cellar, storerooms) and the first floor divided into bedrooms for sleeping. There were no bathrooms, so the stable was also used for one's own bodily needs. The houses, usually square-shaped without porches or terraces, had four to six rooms on the first floor, each of which was assigned to one family or shared by several children. It was not unusual that cousins slept in the same room, if not in the same bed. The family bond was so strong that even cousins were called "brothers". Even if the war had taken many men from their houses and beds, the families still remained numerous.

"There were about 18 people living in our house – three families plus an unmarried uncle – and we talked about

these things all the time. The farm we owned was large and needed many people to work on it." (see Renzo Zocchi)

"During the war we had a landlord and there were 14 of us: a married uncle with three children, [my] Dad with four children and my married brother with another three." (Enrico Marziali*)*

". . . and the family expanded to 30 people." (Cesare Viozzi)

The women

Perhaps for the first time in the history of Italy the women, in the absence of skilled men away engaged in the war, took full responsibility for the family and management of agricultural activity. Houses and land were usually subject to a sharecropping regime: a contract that obliged the peasants to maintain a certain level of productivity, under penalty of expulsion from the land.[7] The women were forced to replace men not only in their traditional work in the vegetable garden but also in the management of the stable and the fields, of the sowing and of the harvests. In fact, traditionally the economy of the house was rigorously administered by a woman, *la vergara,* generally a grandmother who everyone respected and who kept a strict watch on the comings and goings in the house. Due to their leading role in the home, women were the real instigators of the welcome received by the hunted men. It can be said that the social and political advancement of women (recognition of the right to vote and entry into the world of work), which became a mass phenomenon in the post-war period, had its roots in the female initiatives shown in those tragic days between October 1943 and the spring of 1944, initiatives that showed extraordinary courage.

"One day German soldiers turned up at our house to ask if there were any prisoners, but we said no. 'Sure?' said the officer, in broken Italian. 'Absolutely sure!' my mother answered." (see Superio Marinangeli)

The language

Communication between peasants and escapers took place in spite of the language obstacle. On one side the prisoners did not know Italian, and on the other the *contadini* were completely ignorant of the English language. To make communication even more difficult, the *contadini* themselves had little knowledge of standard Italian, having forgotten what little they might have learned in the few years of school attendance. However, some knew "the other" language, those *contadini* who had returned home from America, having gone through the experience of emigration. Back then it was very convenient to know the slang learned in the popular neighbourhoods of New York because it allowed a connection with the prisoners, establishing some essential communication.

". . . they began to speak in English, a language that she [the mother, returned from America] knew very well and this meant she could understand what they needed." (see Giovanni Pilotti)

Likewise, among the prisoners some had learned a bit of Italian which, in these awkward situations, proved very helpful.

"They could speak a little Italian, just a bit, but they managed to make themselves understood very well. They asked if we had any room for them." (Arduina Rossi)

"One of them spoke Italian quite well but the others didn't, they were only able to say a few words." (Renato Corradini)

"We immediately became friends: we were like brothers. Billy spoke a little Italian and was always polite." (Licinio Licini)

In some cases, particularly useful was the presence of young students who attended high school and were studying English as a second language.

". . . I don't remember how they asked for help. My cousin, Artemio, who is dead now, was studying industrial engineering and knew English. He was the one who spoke to the prisoners and translated what they were saying. We children didn't care what was being said, we just used to be there waiting keenly to see if any sweets would come our way." (Renzo Zocchi)

Most of the time, on the first meeting, gestures and a few stunted words were all that were needed for the *contadini* to understand the needs of the escapers and for the latter to establish the willingness of the *contadini* to help.

"He didn't speak much Italian. It was obvious immediately that he was an educated person." (Amelia Antodicola)

". . . I found myself face-to-face with men in uniform. In faltering Italian they asked me if I could give them something to eat. One of them even asked for a cigarette, but I told him that I didn't smoke." (Renato Corradini)

"He didn't speak Italian but we saw immediately that here was a good person. We children willingly spent time teaching him our language, and he was a quick learner. After a month he already knew so many words that he was able to explain himself and communicate; to make himself understood, at any rate." (Enrico Marziali)

Accommodating the prisoners

The reception of prisoners in small and crowded houses in the countryside altered the habits and upset the equilibrium of the *contadino* families. However, an escaper was a guest, a figure celebrated in popular cultures and often referred to in all religious teaching, including Christianity. The sanctity of the guest required the utmost effort to guarantee comfortable accommodation, in addition to personal safety. The first question, when the family decided to take charge of a stranger on the run, was where to put him in the house. Which bed? In which room? On what floor?

Obviously any empty beds on the first floor represented the best option; otherwise the choice fell on the bed occupied by a boy who, making room for the newcomer, was happy to go back to sleep in the warm bed of his parents.

"At home we put him up in my bedroom." (see Enrico Marziali)

"We put him in a small room upstairs but he ate with us." (Amelia Antodicola)

"One was from New Zealand and the other from Australia. The first was a distinguished person, had a slim physique and seemed in poor health. My father didn't feel he could make him sleep in the stable and so he gave him my bed, where I usually slept with my brother." (Abramo Marzialetti)

"So we took him home. My mother placed him in my bed, in the room I shared with my brother, whilst I had to sleep with my parents." (Licinio Licini)

But there were also cases where giving a bedroom in the house was dangerous, and then the goal was to improve on the caves or precarious tents in gullies or the scrub in which the escaper had previously been hiding. The important thing was to ensure a certain level of comfort.

"Our parents put up the prisoners in a hut, where farm equipment was usually kept such as the cart, plough and other things. It didn't have a door so they hung up a blanket at the entrance. They were certainly more comfortable there than in the gully. (Renzo Zocchi)

Filippo Ieranò

"Eventually my father decided to put him in the hayloft near the house. The hay was stacked high and he used a ladder to get up to it; moreover, in the case of danger, it could also be an excellent hiding place." (Superio Marinangeli)

Of course, over time, the solutions changed. The Zocchi family initially accommodated the prisoners in the tool shed, but shortly thereafter the cold of winter caused them to arrange pallets in the warmth of the stable. The stable was also a place from where one could easily flee in case of danger.

"Once we had decided to hide him my parents prepared a good hiding place in the stable. And he remained there at least a month, maybe more." (Lino Luciani)

"Despite the problems, we hid them in the stable . . ." (Gino Leoni)

"Anyway, during that terrible winter he remained with us; he was settled in the stable, hidden among the straw where he certainly wouldn't have suffered from the cold." (Renzo Zocchi)

"They were given a crib in the stable, which was hidden by hay and the animals. They came inside with us for meals. They only hid in the stable in the evening, but during the day we were always together." (Cesare Viozzi)

"Some contadini, seeing us, told us to come in and they hid us in the stable. There were five of us: two Americans,

Bob Sullivan of Albany N.Y. and me, and three Poles whose names I don't remember." (Manuel Serrano)

And if the danger was really great, solutions were found further afield in houses hidden out in the backwoods while still able to provide an acceptable level of comfort. From there the prisoners could still return to the family house to share meals, sitting at the table with other members of the family.

". . . they didn't stay to sleep with us: it was much too dangerous. In Cese there was an earthquake-damaged house, just outside the village, which still offered decent shelter and a few sticks of furniture, like beds and tables. And that was where Dad brought the four Americans, recommending that they stay hidden during the day, but also not to worry because there were no spies in Cese." (Diva Papiri)

"The prisoners lived in out-of-the-way abandoned houses, away from the roads, maybe hidden in the woods, but they had beds, blankets, clothes and all the essentials for living, of course provided by the contadini." (Giovanni Pilotti)

Many families who could not offer accommodation in the house for logistical reasons agreed instead to provide food to a particular prisoner hidden in the woods.

"We didn't have any prisoners in my house because we were too close to the road, but we gave them lots of stuff to eat and to clothe themselves. I remember Jack and John who often came to eat with us." (Neno Brugnolini)

In Montegiorgio, the Marzialetti family was too close to the main road, where German vehicles were constantly coming and going, but they still offered a welcome, building a makeshift shelter in the centre of a woodpile.

"My father built a sort of cage out of strong wooden planks, big enough to 'accommodate' two people. He covered it with a waxed sheet, leaving a hole so that they could enter on all fours." (Abramo Marzialetti)

A network of solidarity

Providing shelter, even if just within a close-knit family, was not a lonely and unsupported exercise. A sort of solidarity network spontaneously grew up, first among the ranks of relatives, then of friends and finally of neighbours. The various activities were thus shared. Families provided food and also kept watch. Those in the houses nearest the streets were used as sentries who alerted the others to any dangers, triggering a prepared escape plan involving inaccessible places in ravines and gullies. If there was then a Nazi-Fascist round-up, everyone was alert to locate and conceal any sign of an escaper's presence. The basic aims of providing shelter were safety, health and comfort. The network also operated to avoid particular burdens on a single family: efforts had to be shared.

"A neighbour called Amedeo Catallo came across four of them at his door asking to be put up. He tried to settle them among different families but couldn't find a place

for one of them. One evening he turned up at our house – we knew him well because he had worked some days with us – and said: 'I can't take three. I've fixed up one, you take another so at least that takes care of two of them!'" (see Enrico Marziali)

"A few days later we agreed to share them out with some families from Cese, one for each. This decision was arrived at because five people were really too many to feed, especially at that time." (Diva Papiri)

"There were 10 people living in our little house so there was no room for prisoners as well. So we spoke to our neighbour who lived just below us because we knew that he had a room. We asked if he would let them sleep there and then they could come to our house to eat. So that's how we arranged it: at night they were at the neighbour's and during the day they were with us." (Renato Corradini)

"Word of their presence quickly got around the neighbourhood and, to avoid the burden falling solely on one family, many others took turns to feed them. So, one time they would come to our house, on another they would go to one of our neighbours." (Licinio Licini)

"For several days prisoners arrived in the village, but they were taken into the countryside by the contadini, to keep them hidden. In the evenings they could generally move about more safely and they went back into the village to meet up and talk amongst themselves." (Amelia Antodicola)

First impressions

The ex-prisoners on the run had endured days of perilous insecurity and their appearance betrayed all their feelings of uncertainty and even despair. Even if they were unable to describe their emotions and desires in words, the *contadini* only needed their eyes to see the condition they were in, down to the smallest detail. The Anglo–Americans were generally tall, accustomed to a protein-rich diet and living in homes certainly cleaner and more comfortable than those of the *contadini*, on whose doors they so desperately knocked. But the world that they had grown up in was now far away. When they approached the poor peasant houses, they were people already tested by hardship.

"They were in bad shape. My mother, when she went to get their things after they'd changed clothes, noticed that they were full of lice, which infested the room. To get rid of them we had to wash everything in boiling water . . ." (see Renato Corradini)

It didn't take long for the contadini to form the impression that the escapers were people worthy of respect.

"Besides that, he was very clean, a bucket of water was enough for him to wash himself. In those days there were no bathrooms and while washing in the bedroom he never spilled a drop." (Enrico Marziali)

". . . they were always respectful and polite." (Renato Corradini)

". . . [he] was always polite and well-mannered . . . he was a handsome boy and tall, typically English." (Amelia Antodicola)

Differences

If in the first contact the linguistic differences formed a barrier that was difficult but not impossible to overcome, the cultural differences appeared a less easy problem to solve. First, if the stay became too long, the different eating habits of the escapers presented an irreconcilable problem. Educating their taste was the most difficult aspect. Sometimes the *contadini* would let their guests get their hands on the pots and pans, just to make fun of them and confirm their belief that neither the Americans nor the British understood good food.

"In American cuisine, he said, milk was used in salads rather than oil." (see Enrico Marziali)

"I would say that the only pleasant, relaxing and in fact hilarious moments were during lunch, which was almost always based on home-made spaghetti. They couldn't roll the blessed spaghetti around the fork; they never managed it, always ending by picking it up with their hands. That caused much hilarity." (Abramo Marzialetti)

In a mirror image, the English and Americans expressed doubts about the habits of the contadini.

". . . they came from a more advanced country than ours, and so they viewed us with somewhat critical eyes,

perhaps sardonic or perhaps, at times, deliberately teasing us." (Diva Papiri)

Religious affiliation could also lead to differences of opinion. The escapers were mainly Protestants and observed with a certain scepticism the religious practices followed by the ordinary people. Although there was still mutual respect.

"With Arturo we talked about religion – in the evening, by the fireplace – and he told us to believe in God. Once, while we were dealing with the oxen, he got flicked in the face by a tail. The flick of the tail is like a whip. He said a word I had never heard and it worried me. I asked him what he had said in American, and he confessed: "I have never cursed God but that just came out!" (Enrico Marziali)

Some prisoners, however, did not hide some sort of cultural and historical presumption that was inherent in the Anglo-Saxon culture, according to which they were the inheritors of a superior civilization. Indeed, some considered the Italians an inferior, subordinate people.

The English, in particular, did not hide their conviction of belonging to a superior people, capable of building the greatest empire in history. Others, however, developed a deep respect for the simple *contadini*, prepared to risk everything they had just to help them.

"There were two English prisoners, Jack and John, the latter housed with the teacher Pia, who came to serious blows in the cantina in Curetta because one said that they were now the masters, since Italy had lost the war, while

the other objected that our families, all of the people, treated them as if they were sons and brothers." (Neno Brugnolini)

Working on the farm

When the fleeing Allied prisoners entered the houses of the peasants, the parallel war announced by Mussolini was already a failure. The Italian army, engaged on the far-away fronts of Russia, Africa and the Balkans, while still fighting alongside the Germans, was in a decidedly subordinate role. The defeats between the end of 1942 and the beginning of 1943 (El Alamein and Stalingrad) and the beginning of the retreat illuminated the political failures of fascism and the military responsibility of the commanders. The fascist regime had desired war, after a period of "non-belligerence", in the hope of sitting with the victors at a peace table which would have redesigned the whole of Europe. War was preferred despite the evidently inadequate conditions of the Italian army compared with the technologies deployed by Hitler's Germany and the Allies. The military High Command gave up on its responsibilities of leadership and protection of their troops. It appeared completely subservient to the will of the Duce.

But a few months later the personal ambitions of Mussolini and the collective ones of the fascist hierarchy had to deal with reality. In defeat, the Italian army also demonstrated the lack of any strategy, with retreats often turning into a rout, with thousands of men captured by the Allies and sent to distant prison camps. However, if squaring one's own conscience could be postponed indefinitely, history was not going to wait. Within a few months Italy lost all its African colonies and in June 1943 suffered the affront of the invasion of Sicily and the slow advance of the Allies. Faced with this political and military failure, at a meeting on 25 July 1943 the Grand Council of Fascism voted for its own demise. Fascism imploded and its body politic was beheaded by the deposing of Mussolini. The same day, the Duce was arrested by order of the king.

As well as this political suicide brought about by the evident collapse of each military objective, there was also a failure to take any responsibility on the part of the military High Command, which instead merely transferred its incompetent allegiance to the king. Some of the hierarchy, such as Marshal Badoglio, took up positions in the king's government.

In a shattered Italy, thousands of families waited anxiously for the end of the war and the return home from prison camps of the thousands of their menfolk. In particular, the houses of the *contadini* suffered from the absence of men to work and carry out the many and continuous activities that agriculture requires. And, even with women trying to replace them, the many difficulties meant that the need for manpower was far in excess of their efforts. As a result the harvests decreased and the land was abandoned.

This was the situation when the former Allied prisoners arrived. Faced with women, old men and boys dealing with the animals, both in the stables or yoked to the plough working the hard clay land, the prisoners got stuck in.

"They were very helpful and, if there was something to do, happy to be useful. To start with they did a lot of the

hoeing, and for the time they stayed with us they never slackened off." (see Renzo Zocchi)

". . . they got organised and made themselves useful, to carry out any chore that allowed them to express their gratitude and to occupy their time. On these occasions, staying on to eat at the house, they strengthened the ties of friendship." (Giovanni Pilotti)

But goodwill, though much appreciated by the *contadini*, wasn't sufficient. In America and England the percentage of farmers in the population was really low. In those countries the great transformation which led to the urbanisation of the 20th century was already well under way. These processes led to widespread land consolidation, mechanisation of production and the disappearance of the small peasant property. The agricultural policy in the Tenna Valley, on the other hand, served to block any internal migration or any political or trade union movements aimed at the emancipation of that world, still subject as it was to the constraints of the sharecropping contract. For many prisoners, therefore, agricultural work was something new, and, for the few who came from the North American countryside or from English hills, that rural world represented a leap into the past. Either way, they were unprepared for the hard manual work that the countryside required.

"They came to work with us. They were willing to help with anything, although they didn't know the country ways. However, little by little they learned and we worked well together, like brothers. We were fond of each other:

they respected us and we respected them." (Arduina Rossi)

But that rural world, simple and basic though it was, also had its charm.

"He worked with us. Yes, indeed. He liked to bring in the oxen and he did everything that was asked of him. In particular, he had the job of fetching water from the well, having rigged up the cart with the cows. He was skilful! Yes, he was good at agricultural work, he really was. He got the hang of things immediately and did everything asked of him." (Lino Luciani)

"In winter there was little work. We could make bundles of firewood but it was not the season for hoeing and you couldn't go into the fields, but they were always willing." (Arduina Rossi)

Of course, not all the escapers were as sensitive.

"All of them joined in the work that the contadini did in the countryside, Albert was the only one who did not step up. Sometimes you'd see him when Dad was chopping wood, but he didn't like to get involved." (Diva Papiri)

Relationships

The sharing of space and the attention to each other's needs fostered deep relationships that verged on friendship, or brotherhood, or that of parent and son. For some that feeling took on a romantic flavour and many were the love affairs that blossomed among the escapers and the women of the valley.

"We had a good relationship with him: he was always very well-mannered. You could see he was a responsible person. He expressed his gratitude and said: 'You are risking a lot for me.'" (see Superio Marinangeli)

"I know of a girl who lived below Amandola who became engaged to a Pole." (Arduina Rossi)

"During that long period a strong relationship arose between the Polish prisoner and my sister Jolanda; in fact, after the war, he returned to marry her and they left together for Argentina, in fact to Buenos Aires." (Luciano Iommi)

The affection was so intense that it led the *contadini* sometimes to "spoil" their guests.

"Everyone liked them, so much so that, on certain occasions, because Robert smoked and it wasn't easy to find cigarettes, an uncle who is now dead went into town and somehow managed to find him some." (Cesare Viozzi)

Unfortunately, within the overall picture of positive feelings there were also unpleasant cases of conflict with the guests as a result of the women of the house. Conflicts that, on a few occasions, led to serious quarrels with tragic outcomes.

"Unfortunately, at Santa Lucia, one of them, a guest in a house, quarrelled with the father and shot him. Perhaps

this was because of a thwarted romance; it seems that he was in love with one of the girls, and the father objected. And, yes, some of the prisoners were also bullies!" (Enrico Marziali)

It also happened that the same events could give rise to different feelings: the prisoners on one hand and the locals on the other. Divisions often arose over the reactions to the bombings carried out by Allied aircraft. For the prisoners, all of this was a cause for joy if not for actual ostentatious enjoyment of that demonstration of power. But not for the peasants! Especially when familiar places were bombed and friends and relatives were killed and/or wounded. Then, having to be both a friend, an ally and an enemy all at the same time was too much to cope with and gave way to feelings of loss on the one hand and pride on the other.

"But there were also moments of tension, such as when my father learned of the death of a friend of his, which occurred at Monte San Martino station. He had cycled just under our house, on his way to take the train for Amandola, and he was strafed by an Allied plane. When we heard the news, Dad cried. The next day, Albert came to lunch and he began to say provocatively: 'I heard important news, our planes have struck again, great, great.'

"Then Dad got angry and said: 'Look, you are an imbecile!'
"'I don't understand, Lorenzo,' he replied looking at him straight in the face.

"'You understand very well!' Dad said. 'You understand what I say. You're making fun of us and our feelings, but remember that if you were a German or a Pole or a fascist or Nazi I would still have done the same as we are doing for you. We do it out of compassion. You could have been anyone. We didn't shelter you because you are American, but because you are in need. Who do you think you are to mock our feelings?'" (Diva Papiri)

Partings

During the months of the German occupation the systematic round-ups meant that many Allied prisoners on the run were captured and deported to labour camps in Germany.

"As time went on we began to hear reports of reprisals and we were afraid that they could come to our house as well and do us harm. In early spring, Charles, aware that the situation was becoming more and more delicate, decided to spend the nights hidden in a cave not far from us. It was in that very hiding place he was taken by the Germans, who deported him to Germany." (see Renzo Zocchi)

In other cases, the prisoners abandoned the families in order to go south, hoping to be reunited with the slowly advancing Allies.

"When the winter was over he left and we never heard from him again. Not while the war was still on, nor afterwards." (Lino Luciani)

When the Allies arrived, most left the houses that had looked after them. On parting, the bonds that had formed were found to be deeper that anyone could have imagined.

"He left us in October of 1946. He stayed with us for two years; even when the Americans came by he didn't want to leave us. Maybe he didn't want to continue the war, maybe he was considered a deserter, I don't know. . . . It wasn't an easy decision for Arturo. He always said: 'Enrico, I'm not going to America, I'm fine with you and I'm staying here!' When he said goodbye to Dad and Mum it was all tears, kisses and hugs. It was unforgettable. I accompanied him to the meeting point and we cried like two babies. An amazing thing!" (Enrico Marziali)

But there were also cases of outright denial of the war, of desertion, to avoid breaking that bond of friendship.

"When the Allies arrived the word went round that the soldiers who had been looked after by families should report to military headquarters at Fermo. Billy went there but returned, saying that he wished to stay here; that this was now his family." (Licinio Licini)

"He didn't want to leave; he must have been with us another couple of months. During that period George was probably regarded as a deserter, and one time he arrived home in a rush, asking for help and a place to hide. We put him down in the hole underneath the barn, where we used to hide supplies. In the meantime, British and Polish

soldiers arrived asking about a man who was on the run."
(Renato Corradini)

Gratitude

The war in the Tenna Valley ended in June 1944. The escapers were assimilated back into civil and military institutions. The Italian government and the UN dealt with the many civilians who had been interned and persecuted and arranged accommodation for them pending their return home or departure to new places. Many among the Jews really wanted to travel to Palestine. The former Allied prisoners rejoined the military ranks and continued to fight or were sent home. Some immediately wrote to their new Italian friends.

"Robert always promised that as soon as the war was over he would come back with the family, and he invited us to go to see him in America. He was a really nice person."
(see Cesare Viozzi)

The following year the war ended on all fronts. The armies demobilised and the soldiers returned to their homes. In the countryside around Servigliano the peasants returned to their usual day-to-day activities, carrying the memory of months passed and friendships established. When everything seemed to be slowly heading back towards normality, the former prisoners began to make spontaneous and entirely personal gestures (in the same way that they had been spontaneously welcomed) to show their gratitude. Letters and parcels began to arrive, followed by visits; first alone, then with wives and children, until old age and death brought them to a close. A lifetime's worth of gratitude.

"We didn't hear anything of him for quite some time and then, a few months after the end of the war, he wrote to us that he was fine and, once again, he thanked us for everything." (Luciano Iommi)

"Albert came back after the war and told us that he had been deported to Germany and then to France. Anyway, thank God, he managed to survive. He often returned to Italy, even when our poor mother died, and every year was different: he came first with his wife, then with children. And more gifts, and many memories." (Diva Papiri)

"Then one day a letter arrived from America. It was Charles writing to thank us. He told us all about his adventures with the Germans who had taken him to Germany, from where he had managed to escape, eventually getting back home to California after the war. From then on we used to write to each other regularly up until two years ago, when my letters to him started to get returned. I have no idea why as I am still receiving his letters. At first Charles also sent us packages with gifts: chocolate, various other stuff and cigarettes. Often, I remember, the packages were tampered with and arrived without cigarettes, and my complaints didn't get me anywhere. Instead, the post office men threatened to have me arrested. Incredible! I invited him to return to Italy. Charles promised that he would come but he hasn't done so yet. But we exchanged photographs: I kept him updated on me and my family, marriage and children,

sending him photos, and he did the same. We have been corresponding for more than 50 years and we are growing old together." (Renzo Zocchi)

There have been those who have returned to Italy, to that valley, to that home to embrace old friends, but also those who did the reverse journey, going to discover the world which lay behind the faces of the former prisoners.

". . . one of the men from my area even found work in America through an ex-prisoner who had been sheltered in his house. I corresponded with some of them and had the opportunity to visit them during my travels in America. I still get Christmas greetings from some of my friends across the ocean." (Giovanni Pilotti)

"When the Allies arrived the word went round that the soldiers who had been looked after by families should report to military headquarters at Fermo. Billy went there but returned, saying that he wished to stay here; that this was now his family. . . . My daughter went to find him during a visit to England. Then he moved to Canada and visits became more difficult, but he still telephones us and is always writing, repeating in Italian: 'If I get to 80 years old, I owe it all to you.'" (Licinio Licini)

As the years rolled by they also brought sad news.

"He began by sending us letters, then one day in the summer of '47 he came with his wife and children. Together we went to see the places where he used to hide; he pointed out to his wife the top of the tower where he

had found shelter during a German raid, and the caves in the countryside.

"We stayed in touch with him for many years, then the letters thinned out until they stopped. But recently, through a granddaughter of mine who knows how to use the internet, we managed to find out that he is dead and that his children live in Venezuela." (Amelia Antodicola)

"They wrote to us periodically for some time, then no more. And so closed a period of our lives, which, for want of a better word, had been really worthwhile." (Abramo Marzialetti)

Not all former sheltered prisoners wrote or returned. Some left a trail of silence.

"Of the three, the only one who wrote after the war was Johnny, who also visited us years ago with his wife and father-in-law. Even now, after such a long time, he continues to send me Christmas greetings and a calendar every year. Still, 50 years later, he sent us this year's 2001 calendar with his greetings." (Renato Corradini)

"We don't know if he's dead or if he's forgotten about us. Let's hope he's forgotten about us." (Superio Marinangeli)

Some made the long journey back only many years later, but memories of faces and conversations were still rekindled.

"I returned to Italy 18 years later and, while I was walking in the countryside around Monte San Martino, I met an

elderly woman and we started talking a bit. She then explained to me that she too had helped an escaped prisoner. I added that there were many prisoners to whom the Italians had given help, but she specified that it was a nurse. I was a nurse! Then I recognised her, 18 years later. . . . Since then almost always I have come back twice a year. I have friends everywhere – Naples, Milan, Rome – but I prefer to return to my valley, between Monte San Martino and Penna San Giovanni, where I hid for the first time." (Keith Killby)

So to whom is this gratitude due?

"We were lucky but we owe a debt of thanks for having survived: first of all to the Allies who bombed the camp, enabling us to flee; also to the partisans as well as to ordinary people like that doctor at Servigliano who advised us to run off; and to Father Galli and the friars." (Carla Viterbo)

"I will never be able to forget how much the Italians helped us! Above all, it was the poorest houses that always tried to give us something." (Keith Killby)

Certificates of merit

At the end of the war the Allied command instigated a system of evaluating the extent of popular mobilisation in support of the more than 50,000 Allied prisoners who, before the arrival of the Germans, fled the camps in Italy and managed to avoid being captured and deported to Germany. Through the accounts of these escapers the High Command also discovered the human dimension of that aid. They came to understand the price that was paid in terms of death and suffering. Decades before historiography made any distinction between armed partisan resistance and unarmed civil resistance, the Allies acknowledged the extraordinary nature of these events and, in order to give them a certificate of merit and a small cash contribution, set up a commission to identify families who had helped Allied prisoners. The commission concluded its work at the end of 1947, identifying about 85,000 families between central and northern Italy. One third (about 25,000) were to be found between the south of Le Marche and the north of Abruzzo. With the usual English punctuality, each house received the certificate and sum of money. In contrast, the Italian state completely ignored those events. After the war, poverty was a given for all of Italy and receiving money was a reason for joy for many of the "deserving".

"Then the Americans decided to make awards to those families who had suffered damage as a result of their generosity; for instance, for that house burned by the Germans near the river Ete. Almost all of them received gifts." (see Neno Brugnolini)

"A little time passed, then, to our amazement and astonishment, the English command sent us about 30,000 lire and a parchment as a token of gratitude for the shelter given to prisoners during the war. Thirty thousand lire were really a lot for us farmers and that money allowed us to pay off some debt, but certainly what we did for the three Englishmen was only to help people in difficulty, with no other ulterior motive." (Renato Corradini)

However, despite the goodwill of the Allies, their gift also caused embarrassment and indignation, both among families who received this lavish and unlooked-for generosity and also among the former Allied prisoners. For families, they were embarrassed that their sheltering of the escapers, so willingly undertaken, could be quantified. Many former Allied prisoners were also indignant. Having experienced the hospitality of those families and their exposure to terrible risks, they wrote to the authorities expressing their bewilderment at the smallness of the sums paid out.[8]

"In 1945 the British, in recognition of those who had sheltered prisoners, gave them a sum of money, but Mum, indignant, immediately turned hers over to a missionary association." (Licinio Licini)

1. The camp at Fossoli, near Modena, was the collection point for Italian Jews. A total of 2,802 were deported from there, mostly to Auschwitz.
2. Formed after the Armistice, the CIL numbered about 300,000 troops of the Italian Royal Army who opted to fight with the Allies, mostly in a non-combat capacity.
3. The Italian Social Republic, known as the Republic of Salò, was a German puppet state set up in northern Italy for Mussolini following his rescue by German troops. His fascist supporters were known as Republicans.
4. More than 90% of those called to the military service in the province of Ascoli, supposedly forming the new army of Salò, did not show up. Draft evasion was widespread and determinedly supported by families.
5. F. Ieranò: *L'eccidio dimenticato*, KDP edition.
6. Supporters of the Republic were known as Republicans.
7. *The contadini* were subject to a regime known as the *mezzadria*. This was a sharecropping scheme in which everything they produced had to be shared 50/50 with their

padrone (landlord). They were mostly illiterate and at the mercy of their *padrone*, who could turn them out for any reason, including if he considered that the family had insufficient able-bodied members to provide the labour for a maximum crop.

8. R. Absalom, A Strange Alliance, Aspects of Escape and Survival in Italy 1943–1945. Florence Accademia Toscana di Scienze Lettere "La Colombaria".

PART THREE

The testimonies

The sometimes fragmentary accounts assembled in this section spring from conversations during which I tried to reconstruct events that had occurred 70 years previously. In transcribing them I have put the story-telling in order while retaining the emotion that the language – a combination of Italian and dialect – sought to convey.

Each conversation was recorded and this enabled me to make the statements coherent by removing the questions and repetitions. I could also accommodate sudden recollections that brought out important points.

On occasions, telling the story was a very emotional experience for the narrator, prompting memories of family members and friends and of suffering and fears that have scarred different generations. For some witnesses, recalling those events was truly liberating. Others, however, were more reticent or were fearful of recounting something trivial, dismissively saying: *"Everybody was kind to the prisoners . . ."*

I hope, however, that the statements give the opportunity to pay tribute to these ordinary people who demonstrated how to act as model citizens.

Renzo Zocchi

He covered himself with mud

Renzo Zocchi

At the time of these events I was around 13 years old. I knew that at Servigliano there was a concentration camp and that prisoners of war were being held there. But I did not know who they were or where they came from. Before the escape on 8 September 1943 I had managed to approach some prisoners because my uncle owned a small piece of land on the south side of the camp, near the boundary wall. A great, tall cherry tree grew there, and, climbing it when the fruit was ripe, I could throw cherries over the wall towards the prisoners. Of course, I was very careful never to do this when the guards were there, or made sure that they were looking the other way. The prisoners, to thank me, threw me some bars of soap. That was probably stuff that they had received in their Red Cross parcels.

A People's Courage

During the springs of 1940 to 1943, when picking the cherries, I often saw prisoners but never the same faces. It was difficult for me to know what nationality they were; I only knew that they were prisoners of war. In the village, people said there were Jewish people, Americans . . . but these were only rumours.

The people of Servigliano, though, were completely disconnected from the life of the camp. Their only involvement was with the guards who spent money in the local shops and attended the bars in the evening. But the locals were totally cut off from the life of the camp.

In September 1943 there occurred the momentous event of the breakout from the camp and the death of a prisoner, shot by a guard. This caused a furore. To be honest, there were stories that people told in the heat of the moment but I have never been able to find out if they really happened.

In those days, news about the Armistice was doing the rounds and we heard of it often on the radio. At home we were happy and thought it would mean no more shooting. There were about 18 people living in our house – three families plus an unmarried uncle – and we talked about these things all the time. The farm we owned was large and needed many people to work on it. We were all convinced that the war was over but, instead, a few days later we saw prisoners arriving in droves along the gully, carrying possessions in rucksacks and under their arms. They were walking in small groups, here and there, doing their best to keep a low profile. That will have been the 9th or 10th of September. Many of them stopped in the fields and cautiously approached the houses. Some of them even gave us some chocolate which for us was heaven. Others made up improvised tents, hidden in the gully, and stayed there for a few days.

I was 13 and in those days it was like being a small child. We hid so that we could spy on them – just the children, obviously, as the adults were too busy working in the fields. The presence of the prisoners was such a novelty. Our parents understood the misery of the prisoners on the run, some of them had also been in the First War and knew what hunger meant or the discomfort of sleeping under the stars, in the cold. I remember my parents gave us loaves of bread, about a kilo, baked in the wood oven, to take to the prisoners hidden in the gully, and in return they gave us some sweets, even cigarettes. So we went there often. We were never short of bread; in the country it was the one thing we always had plenty of.

I don't remember exactly how long they were camped out in the gully, possibly days or weeks. But gradually, as the weather worsened, they began to approach the houses to ask for shelter. Not just in our home, also others in the area, spreading themselves out among different families.

At the beginning there were at least five prisoners at our house: they were English, American and one was Jewish. I have a vague memory that the Jewish man's name was Risorciali – that's how he introduced himself but I can't remember if he was Italian or foreign. He spoke a bit of Italian but my memories are not clear.

The name of the Englishman was Williams, and then there were two Americans who used to come and go, Johnny and Charles. It was hunger that brought them to us and I don't remember how they asked for help. My cousin, Artemio, who is dead now, was studying industrial engineering and knew English. He was the one who spoke to the prisoners and translated what they were saying. We children didn't care what was being said, we just used to be there waiting keenly to see if any sweets would come our way.

Our parents put up the prisoners in a hut, where farm equipment was usually kept such as the cart, plough and other things. It didn't have a door so they hung up a blanket at the entrance. They were certainly more comfortable there than in the gully.

I was impressed by the Englishman, Williams, because he was just how I imagined an Englishman to look: thin, taller than the others, with a lean, athletic build. He only knew a few words of Italian, they communicated with gestures mainly and through Artemio – you can always manage to communicate when you really need to.

They were very helpful and, if there was something to do, happy to be useful. To start with they did a lot of the hoeing, and for the time they stayed with us they never slackened off. Then, because of the round-ups taking place in the area, they went away.

One day the Germans came: suddenly we heard the noise of cars arriving, harsh commands being shouted. The prisoners immediately disappeared back to the gully. The Germans, after they had had a look around the house, set off in pursuit of the prisoners. Among the first to be captured was Williams, who couldn't run because his shoes were hurting him. They put him on a lorry and took him away: we never heard any more about him. The others managed to spread out between the gully and the wood and after a few days we saw them emerge again.

The Germans came back to our house another three times after that.

One day they turned up without us having seen them coming: we were busy building a wall with stones and mud and the Jewish fugitive was helping us. When we heard them they were already 20 metres from the house, and the Jewish fugitive cleverly covered himself in the mud we were using. So when the Germans searched the house for escaped prisoners they didn't find anything out of the ordinary and went away.

Some time later, in the winter, the Jew went away and Johnny found shelter with another family.

During the winter a few other prisoners came to our house – they were always given something to eat and in some cases they stayed for a few days before moving on.

The only one who stayed for a long time was Charles, the American. He must have been in part Chinese or Japanese because he had some Eastern characteristics and had gradually learned a bit of Italian. He told us he came from California, had a farm producing cotton near San Francisco. He invited us to visit him once the war was over.

Charles was a really nice guy and he was always with us, willing to do anything. Unfortunately, just before the Americans arrived, he was captured by the Germans.

Anyway, during that terrible winter he remained with us; he was settled in the stable, hidden among the straw where he certainly wouldn't have suffered from the cold.

He was always ready to do any job but he had his own personal way of working: in fact, to avoid getting a hunch back, he had made himself a hoe with a very long handle so that he could hoe without bending down. We treated him as one of the family and our parents were always ready to help him, out of kindness, as they knew that otherwise he would have been captured or have gone hungry; we were always afraid of the Germans.

As time went on we began to hear reports of reprisals and we were afraid that they could come to our house as well and do us harm. In early spring, Charles, aware that the situation was becoming more and more delicate, decided to spend the nights hidden in a cave not far from us. It was in that very hiding place he was taken by the Germans, who deported him to Germany.

In that cave he wasn't alone either – there were four or five of them who had all been sheltered by local families.

It turned out that a man had gone to the fascists to tell on them: apparently they beat and threatened him as some of the prisoners' possessions were found in his house. But other people said that they were betrayed by someone wanting to pocket the reward money that was on the head of all prisoners on the run.

Anyway, it was easy for the Germans, with these tip-offs, to surprise them in the grotto at night and capture them.

These were difficult times because there were ever-increasing partisan attacks on the Nazi-Fascists; at home there were lots of anti-war sentiments expressed and people were persuaded that it was right to help the prisoners on the run. Not that we thought too much about the risks: we couldn't but help them, poor things!

Events were really frightening for everyone. Near here, on the main road, partisans attacked and blew up a German lorry. The next day the Germans descended in force and beat up the people who lived near the road, damaging some of the houses. On one occasion they humiliated a man called Misiri, who lived in the house next to the church of Saint Gualtiero, making him drag a horse cart with several Germans on it. However, luckily there were no fatal attacks or injuries in the area. The Germans would come round here and then go on to the village. The fascists, though, never showed their faces – they stayed hidden.

We knew a partisan in Santa Vittoria and one in Fermo and I volunteered to carry packages for them, travelling from Fermo to San Gualtiero by train and then on to my house where someone from Santa Vittoria would come and pick them up. The packages contained dismantled weapons but at the age of 13, even though I knew what was in them, I didn't pay much heed to the risk involved.

There were also people who passed themselves off as *"patriotti"* (partisans) and whom we called *"ladriotti"* (petty thieves). They went from house to house at night asking for money and threatening people. The worst episode happened at Belmonte: some people knocked at the door of a house at Squarcia and when the wife opened the door they told her they were partisans in need of money. When the terrified woman slammed the door shut immediately they threw a hand grenade at the door but it was only damaged, not destroyed.

That door, patched up a bit in places, continued to work perfectly well for a long time. I used to see it every time I went to Belmonte. Just a few days ago I noticed that it had been replaced.

After Charles had been captured we didn't hear any news from him for a long time. Then one day a letter arrived from America. It was Charles writing to thank us. He told us all about his adventures with the Germans who had taken him to Germany, from where he had managed to escape, eventually getting back home to California after the war. From then on we used to write to each other regularly up until two years ago, when my letters to him started to get returned. I have no idea why as I am still receiving his letters. At first Charles also sent us packages with gifts: chocolate, various other stuff and cigarettes. Often, I remember, the packages were tampered with and arrived without cigarettes, and my complaints didn't get me anywhere. Instead, the post office men threatened to have me arrested. Incredible!

I invited him to return to Italy. Charles promised that he would come but he hasn't done so yet. But we exchanged photographs: I kept him updated on me and my family, marriage and children, sending him photos, and he did the same. We have been corresponding for more than 50 years and we are growing old together.

From a conversation with Renzo Zocchi (born 1930); San Gualtiero, Servigliano, August 1999

Sandro Kanzaghi

They soon began to fight each other

In 1940, when Greeks and Greek-Cypriots were starting to be interned, I was sent to Servigliano as an interpreter, but I ended up being involved in everything from the infirmary to the kitchen. The prisoners were grouped in separate barracks, each with an officer who represented them. There were also English, American, French and even Polish prisoners there. This had been the case since 1943.

Colonel Bacci, the camp commandant, gave me the job of passing messages between the authorities and the prisoners. I remember I was in Turin studying languages when I was called to the Ministry of the Interior because I knew other languages, especially Greek, which was my native tongue. I was, in fact, born in Rhodes and moving from that small island to a big city like Turin and then to Rome which made quite an impression on me.

At the ministry they said they needed an interpreter who knew Greek and English well: I told them I also knew French and a bit of German.

When I arrived at Servigliano I was around 22 years old. I was put to work straight away by Commandant Bacci, who was having great difficulty communicating with the prisoners. He was an elderly man, very cultured, who had been in charge of the camp for the duration of the war.

At the beginning the camp received around 1,600 prisoners and in my opinion the conditions were not particularly hard; of course, it was still a prisoner of war camp! All the same, I established very cordial relations with the prisoners. I remember that when the English prisoners were digging an escape tunnel I saw what they were doing but said nothing. They were digging under the raised floor of the barracks, and they were piling up the earth in the cavity wall. Eleven of them managed to escape and the guards only noticed the next morning at roll call.

The local people were well disposed towards the prisoners and the rules of the camp were not rigid. Some prisoners went out every morning to do the shopping, always accompanied by guards; some went out to work for the *contadini* and they were happy to do it as they always got something in return. The same prisoners used to ask to go and work outside the camp, and if someone needed to be punished they would not be allowed to go.

In Servigliano in those days there was a lack of men to work the land because the farmworkers were away fighting, so people appreciated the willingness of the prisoners to help out and they got to know them. Local inhabitants, guards and prisoners all used to bargain and exchange goods because the prisoners received Red Cross parcels every month that contained many items which were no longer available to us, such as coffee, top-quality cigarettes, chocolate, perfumed soap and so on. These products were exchanged for basic foods such as bread, cheese and other things. For the prisoners these parcels were a real godsend because they provided many things they lacked in the camp and also helped them make friends.

I also used to take some things from the prisoners but I didn't have anything to give them in return. So I handed them money that they could use in the camp shop, which kept a lot of stock.

This exchange was not legal but everyone did it so it was allowed. After the break-out from the camp on 8 September 1943 many prisoners sought out the families they already knew to ask for help. They ended up hiding in the houses of families for whom they had already worked.

I was not there when the break-out happened because I had been sent to be an interpreter at Poppi, near Bibbiena, not far from Florence, where there was a prisoner of war camp for Greek officers and non-commissioned officers. I had outgrown my usefulness at Servigliano anyway because the prisoners had by then learned enough Italian to communicate and they were able to help each other. It was Commandant Bacci who told me I was going to be sent to Poppi for a while, because the authorities were having a very difficult time with the Greek prisoners who were constantly demanding their rights but could not make themselves understood.

On 8 September all the prisoners in Poppi also broke out of the camp, as did many of the guards. I decided to return to Servigliano, not because I was asked to but because I had got to know a girl there who would later become my wife.

When I arrived in Servigliano I saw that the prisoners had escaped and only a few soldiers remained in charge of the camp, as many of them had set off for their homes. One of them, a man from Padua, was later found dead not far away: he had fled the camp intending to return home and had hidden himself, to no avail, with a family of *contadini*.

My girlfriend told me that, a few days after the break-out at the Armistice, a Carabinieri marshal had ordered this man to be hunted down and they were going on a house-to-house search. This marshal had also been to her family home and taken away a lot of things that had come from the prisoners, saying that they belonged to the camp. I had been given some coffee, tea and other things by the prisoners that I had then given to my girlfriend. This was just one of many very upsetting experiences.

That marshal was worse than a Nazi. He put the fear of God into everyone and imposed a curfew on Servigliano in order to try and recapture the prisoners and any other non-fascists. He had taken control of the whole area.

It was during that time that a Greek man, who had been taken in by a local family, was killed. They had discovered he was there and had surrounded the house at night to arrest him. He had jumped out of the window to escape down the slope above the district of Terrabianca, just outside the village, but a policeman opened fire and shot him. Under darkness, the poor man still tried to make his escape and his cries could be heard for many hours until the morning when the Carabinieri, continuing their search, found his dead body. I think the whole of Servigliano will have heard the Greek's cries of pain but nobody was brave enough to go to his aid for fear of getting shot, such was the prevailing climate of fear. There should be a plaque in his memory here in the cemetery where he was buried. He had sought refuge with a family but unfortunately he had been discovered.

My wife's family, too, were helping two Americans, one of whom had a gunshot wound in his arm after being hit by one of the guards on the day of the break-out. They lived in a small house near the camp, which was by then deserted. One evening the leader of the fascists at Servigliano happened to call in at my girlfriend's house, with several Carabinieri. Waving a pistol in my face he demanded that I tell him if they were hiding prisoners. I responded in a way he didn't like and he suddenly let off a shot with his pistol that luckily just missed me.

The two prisoners only came to my girlfriend's house at night to eat and collect some things before setting off again to wherever they were hiding. Occasionally they stayed the night because the one who had been shot was in a bad way. They told us they had found shelter in an abandoned haystack. They stayed in the area for a few weeks before announcing that they were going to try to join the partisan units in the mountains. We never heard what happened to them after that.

In the meantime the Germans had settled in, helping themselves to anything they wanted from the camp stores. Almost every evening we heard gunshots and I don't think the Greek was the only person killed in Servigliano. But news did not get passed around: we were frightened and nobody asked questions. The marshal had created a real atmosphere of terror in order to defend the stores. But the Germans couldn't have cared less about the stores because they had already emptied them of everything they could possibly use.

All the same, conditions were very difficult and desperate people were risking their lives trying to get anything they could from the stores. I remember that it was the Carabinieri who shot at people, not the Germans.

I believe it was during one of those raids on the stores that a woman was killed. As far as I know, the woman really did die but the marshal denied all knowledge of it.

In the spring of 1944 the partisans also started to make their presence felt in the area: two German soldiers were killed very close to the village walls. There was mounting tension over the following few days, with the Germans wanting to carry out a reprisal by killing 20 local inhabitants. Fortunately I managed to convince one woman who spoke German, like me, and who was friends with the German commandant, to go with me to see him and explain that the partisans could not have been local. I remember that I didn't sleep that night in order to give the appearance of being ill. I had this idea in my head that it would help me avoid capture: who would have dared to kill a sick man? After the meeting the commandant decided to let it go and there were no reprisals. This was all the woman's doing – I was just there to provide back-up.

Another attack happened on the road in front of the church of Saint Gualtiero: it was a column of four or five vehicles and probably quite a few more were killed.

In the summer the first English people started to make an appearance: they were telegraphers who were immediately taken on as interpreters. Being in their company I was able to witness the rapid unfolding of events. The Germans had already left the village a few days before and the situation was very uncertain. The partisans started carrying out vendettas. The wife of a fascist was beaten and had her head shaved in the square, while her husband had fled. Everyone was afraid because you only had to be accused of having collaborated with the Germans to find yourself in danger. Personal animosity became political hatred. Even I was afraid of being accused of collaboration because I had worked as an interpreter at the camp. Luckily I had quickly started working with the English after that and no-one made any accusations against me.

It was in the square that the famous punch-up took place between the marshal of the Carabinieri and a former prisoner of the camp called Manuel Serrano. He must have gone off into the mountains to join the partisans after the camp break-out and, one day, when visiting Servigliano, he met the marshal as he was coming out of the bar. Serrano immediately started to yell at him: "Do you remember?" He was shouting about all the bullying and harassment he had been subjected to and it wasn't long before they started punching each other. People were shouting "Well done, Serrano!", which just showed the extent to which the marshal was universally loathed. Serrano was a strong man and he was getting the upper hand when suddenly we heard the sound of little girls' voices calling for their daddy – it was the marshal's daughters. Their cries stopped Serrano in his tracks and he let go of the marshal and stood looking at him lying at his feet covered with blood. Shortly afterwards the marshal was taken to hospital in Fermo but he turned out not to be badly hurt.

At that stage I had to go away to serve elsewhere, but I was still worried because my girlfriend's father was a signed-up member of the Fascist Party. Some people who had believed in Mussolini at the beginning slowly began to grasp the disaster he had created and many of them changed their minds.

From a conversation with Sandro Kanzaghi (born 1918); Servigliano, August 1999

Enrico Marziali

It was impossible to refuse a bit of bread

I was born in this house and have lived here for 76 years. The house was built the same year that work began to renovate Servigliano downstream.

During the war we had a landlord and there were 14 of us: a married uncle with three children, [my] Dad with four children and my married brother with another three. Our grandparents had passed away. As for my family, it consisted of two boys and two girls in addition to our parents.

When war broke out I was about 17 years old and I remember lots of things pretty well, first and foremost the poverty. There were so many taxes to pay, debt payments in particular, and then there was produce to give to the landlord. The land wasn't big enough to make do and, through day jobs elsewhere, we tried to earn something in order to improve the situation. Of course, this wasn't permanent employment, it was only day labour.

We also had animals at home and there was no shortage of work. But we didn't produce enough for the number that we were: there were too many mouths to feed. Here almost all the families were large ones and they had to cope in the same way that we did. The war had certainly made things worse because earlier – and I'm referring to the beginning of the 1930s – the situation in the countryside hadn't been so grim. Then Mussolini embarked on building an empire and, that not being enough for him, he allied himself with Germany to conquer the world. Mussolini had gone mad, because war is just madness. He wanted everything and we were reduced to eating bread made of corn and bran.

Two of my close relatives were called up at the outbreak of war: one of them, Vincenzo, my blood brother, joined the guards at Servigliano concentration camp; the other, my cousin, was sent to Yugoslavia.

We knew little about the camp. Vincenzo was a cook, not a guard, and he didn't have contact with the prisoners. We knew somehow that there were lots of prisoners and that they were guarded by the soldiers.

We also got to hear that the prisoners had attempted an escape by digging tunnels but that they had been recaptured.

In September 1943 news of the Armistice caused a general dispersal but we were happy. The guards opened the camp for the prisoners, telling them to make do for themselves, and they left to go home; and Vincenzo came here.

At the time the Germans were coming and going and if they had got hold of them inside the camp they would have shot them all.

Thousands of prisoners scattered throughout the valley.

When Sesto, the cousin in Yugoslavia, got to hear of the Armistice he too tried to escape like everybody else. But he didn't attempt to return home, that was too far away even to think of it; he joined Tito's partisans. Unfortunately, during a round-up by the Germans, he was captured and taken to Germany for four months before being freed by the Russians.

At home, in our hamlet, some prisoners approached families for help. A neighbour called Amedeo Catallo came across four of them at his door asking to be put up.

He tried to settle them among different families but couldn't find a place for one of them. One evening he turned up at our house – we knew him well because he had worked some days with us – and said: "I can't take three. I've fixed up one, you take another so at least that takes care of two of them!"

He knew what sort of people we were and we replied: "Bring him, whoever he is! One more mouth to feed won't matter!"

My brother, Vincenzo, who had left the camp, was a bit worried. "We're taking risks," he said. "It's a big responsibility and I really wouldn't want that."

"We've got Sesto in Yugoslavia," I replied, "and we haven't had news of him for so long. Don't you think it's possible someone has sheltered him?" I added: "It's almost a matter of conscience."

Eventually he too agreed.

Of course, we had to see what the prisoner was like, given that there were already so many of us. However, it was impossible to refuse a bit of bread to somebody in those circumstances. So Amedeo brought him here. When he entered the house he was wearing a military jacket and had nothing else.

He was tall, with a thin face and blond hair above a broad forehead; he was beginning to go bald above the temples. He was about 26 or 27 years old and he told us his name was Arturo, Arturo Schupper, an American from Pennsylvania. He didn't speak Italian but we saw immediately that here was a good person.

We children willingly spent time teaching him our language, and he was a quick leaner. After a month he already knew so many words that he was able to explain himself and communicate; to make himself understood, at any rate.

Besides that, he was very clean, a bucket of water was enough for him to wash himself. In those days there were no bathrooms and while washing in the bedroom he never spilled a drop.

He was also a good worker, ready for anything and by our side whatever we were doing. Not that he was a farmer like us: he explained that he worked in a timber firm that constructed wooden houses. He was well off; he showed us photos of the car he had at home, something that we could only dream of.

For fun he sometimes spoke in American, but we didn't understand him and would start laughing. I only remember the numbers, and not even all of them: "One, two, tree, foor." To be honest, there wasn't even time to joke. No, there wasn't!

Arturo never complained. He ate with pleasure everything that the women cooked, even though he had strange tastes. In American cuisine, he said, milk was used in salads rather than oil.

We tried to get him something to smoke because he was very keen on smoking. Naturally we had to get him some clothes. At home we put him up in my bedroom; there was Arturo, Vincenzo and myself. The room was quite spacious and all three of us could sleep there.

To start with he met up with comrades staying with other families, but then he began to distance himself from them. He saw that others were not as well placed as he was and that this could cause jealousy.

Besides, not all the prisoners were good like Arturo. Unfortunately, at Santa Lucia, one of them, a guest in a house, quarrelled with the father and shot him. Perhaps this was because of a thwarted romance; it seems that he was in love with one of the girls, and the father objected. And, yes, some of the prisoners were also bullies!

In truth we risked a lot to look after Arturo at home. However, we had in mind the cousin in Yugoslavia from whom we hadn't had a letter, nor received any news, for months. We were hoping that he was in the same situation as Arturo, that he was being helped. Perhaps he was already being looked after by some family or other.

Certainly there was enormous danger. I remember we were in bed one evening when we heard the sound of shooting from the road, which was about 500 metres away. We immediately thought of the fascists. Arturo bolted into the fields to hide and I cautiously approached the road to find out what was happening: I saw some people cutting the telephone wires. Hearing a voice I thought I recognised I went up to them and asked what they were doing.

"We've got to cut all communications here, we're partisans," they replied.

So I went back home and tracked Arturo down in order to reassure him and bring him back.

There was a time when the fascists came along at night checking for prisoners, house by house. That was when we had to ask Arturo to move out and hide in the scrub near the river Ete. After a couple of days he came back to get something to eat and, I admit, I wept to see him so downcast. How happy he was when I went to call him back home because the danger had passed. His face lit up as if it were a lamp regaining its power.

However, Arturo himself was well aware of the need to slip away, because he really didn't want to risk being captured. When there were checks Dad would tell him:

"We'll get food to you but you must sort out where you're going to sleep. Meanwhile, let's see how things go."

Fortunately, after a few days, the storms subsided, the danger ceased and he returned home. The risk, however, was really great. But we were not naïve; there was enough communication between the families who had the prisoners for news of any danger to get around immediately.

The winter was tough but we did okay because we had enough wood. In the evening we would be all together at home. Once or twice I took him to Curetta, but he told me: "Enrico, I like to come round but it's not good for me to see so many people, word could get out."

He was aware of the danger and wanted to avoid it. He said: "I'm fine with you and I don't want to cause trouble!"

I don't know if he was a Catholic, he certainly didn't go to church. However, after he returned to America we received a package that contained a Bible: it belonged to his sister, who was apparently a nun. I still remember that Don Ottavio from Curetta, knowing that this Bible had arrived, sent for me and told me that I could not keep it.

"Why?" I asked.

"Because it is forbidden," he answered. Actually, in those days nobody had one and when someone asked me if I kept it I denied it. We were church people and we still are, except that today everyone has the Bible while in the past it was not like that.

With Arturo we talked about religion – in the evening, by the fireplace – and he told us to believe in God. Once, while we were dealing with the oxen, he got flicked in the face by a tail. The flick of the tail is like a whip. He said a word I had never heard and it worried me. I asked him what he had said in American, and he confessed: "I have never cursed God but that just came out!" It happened only that one time.

Arturo was really like a member of the family, and when he left everyone was in tears. I accompanied him to the meeting point; he hugged me so tight that we cried bitter tears.

He was such a good and respectful person that I have never seen the like again. Always ready to work. If we needed to feed the animals he would ask: "How much do I give them?"

He learned quickly when we showed him. He was always ready to do any work, dealing with the hay, wheat or whatever. He was always there.

Everyone loved him. But he and I were like two brothers, he was always close to me. I told him, jokingly, that it seemed like he was in love with me.

He left us in October 1946. He stayed with us for two years; even when the Americans came by he didn't want to leave us. Maybe he didn't want to continue the war, maybe he was considered a deserter. I don't know.

Of the many prisoners who were in the surrounding area in 1943, only a few remained. Then in 1946 came the news that all Americans could return to their homeland and that trucks were coming to pick them up.

It wasn't an easy decision for Arturo. He always said: "Enrico, I'm not going to America, I'm fine with you and I'm staying here!" When he said goodbye to Dad and Mum it was all tears, kisses and hugs. It was unforgettable. I accompanied him to the meeting point and we cried like two babies. An amazing thing!

He felt safe in our home and feared he would have trouble leaving. We stayed in contact for many years,

Filippo Ieranò

thanks to the help of a teacher from Curetta who knew English and translated the letters for us. Maybe until the seventies. And we knew that he was married, that he had a daughter. He sent us photographs. He got himself a new car. There was less contact after the teacher moved away, leaving us with a problem of translating from English. Sometimes we turned to Vecchiotti, a councillor, but all of a sudden the correspondence stopped.

I think about him every day and I'm glad I did what I did. Of course, we took a risk, but we soon realised that he was someone who was worth it.

A few months after Arturo's departure, while I was hunting near the river Ete, I heard Aunt Gigia call me. I went up to her and she told me that, on leaving the first Mass, in Curetta, they had seen Sesto.

Could it be true? I raced home and hugged him. He said he had been a prisoner in Germany and he looked like a toothpick because they fed him a potato a day. One potato!

He was freed by the Russians, who took him to Russia, treated him and restored him to health: he ate five times a day. To look at him he wasn't recognisable anymore: he became a round ball. All his clothes had to be remade.

Best wishes to you all.

From an interview with Enrico Marziali (born 1923); Servigliano, September 1999

Diva Papiri

The fascists searched the houses, armed with submachine guns

I lived in Cese di Montefalcone with my family. Mother was a teacher and my father came from Cese. I also had a grandmother in Montefalcone who lived alone after the death of my grandfather. And, of course, we had family farther away in the area.

The village was only small and our house was a short way outside it, but close to other houses.

In 1943 I was 18 and I remember very well what happened. I was studying at Fermo high school, but my mother wanted to take me out of school, advising me to take the teaching diploma so that I would not have to go to university. While everything was happening, I was studying as a private student at home.

In July I went to Ascoli to take my exams, accompanied by my father. There was no transport and Dad decided we were going to go by bike. We arrived in the town, which had not yet been occupied by the Germans, and Dad stayed with me for a week to allow me to take all the tests. At the end of the week we picked up our bikes again. "So, let's take a trip anyway," said Dad. That is such a strong memory, our return from Ascoli: the sun, the fields, the climbs. . . .

A few weeks later came news of the Armistice. I cried with happiness, so much emotion! In a few days many of those who had been called up returned; they arrived on foot, tired and dirty, passing through the fields to get home as soon as possible. And when the news spread of someone's return there were kisses and tears, even the church bell rang in celebration.

In those days the confrontation between fascists and partisans became fiercer. I had a relative, his name was Papiri, a partisan who had a radio transmitter with which he contacted the Allies, and he often came to our house. Dad was very worried and concerned that the fascists might come and hurt me. There was also a rumour that there was a particular connection between me and that boy, but it was not true: it was just friendship.

Papiri managed to organise a band of partisans and he said that he had received weapons dropped by parachutes by the Allies. Sometimes I was curious to listen to the radio, because I knew it used a language in code that made little sense. Still, they certainly managed to get weapons, because they were all armed. The objective of this band was also to defend the boys born in 1925, the last class that had been called up. Because of the Armistice they did not sign up at the headquarters where they were supposed to go, thus rendering themselves deserters. These boys were in hiding because the fascists were looking for them, also using spies to find and arrest them. One day some trucks full of soldiers arrived and one of my neighbours, who was wanted, came to seek shelter with us. Mother hid him under the floor of the barn, where there was a hatch that led into a cave, and she covered everything with straw and hay.

I remember Mum used to shuttle from one part of the house to another to secretly watch the movements of the fascists who were searching houses, armed with machine guns and as bold as brass. My poor mother was determined, but also frightened to think that they might discover the boy's hiding place. But it didn't happen: they came in, but did not search the house thoroughly and then they went away again.

Since the Armistice there had been news of the prisoners escaping. Rumours circulated that the guards had opened the gates of the prison camps of Servigliano and of Monte Urano. It was known that in the woods around Montefalcone there were several of them, but I hadn't ever seen any. One evening in the autumn – it was rainy and cold – Dad, who was a hunter, went "on call", a kind of stakeout that they did to trap birds returning to their nests. All of a sudden he heard noises behind a hedge. He drew close and saw four people, dressed in thin, worn-out clothes. Dad got scared, but the others were frightened too.

They raised their hands, saying: "We Americans, friends, we're friends."

They must have been there a long time.

Dad asked them: "How long have you been here?"

"For days, for days. We hungry, we are hungry," they answered.

Then Dad told them to follow him, that he would make his way to the village to get food for them.

When they got home Mum was shocked at their poor state: they had frightened faces, long beards and soaked, dirty clothes. They must have been in the area for a while without being able to find shelter or food.

Mum lit a big fire to dry them out and Dad gave them things to wear, since they had no change of clothes.

Mum quickly prepared the pasta and they enjoyed it, even if it was not their normal food: they definitely preferred meat, potatoes and desserts, as they told us later.

We fed them for two or three days, but they didn't stay to sleep with us: it was much too dangerous. In Cese there was an earthquake-damaged house, just outside the village, which still offered decent shelter and a few sticks of furniture, like beds and tables. And that was where Dad brought the four Americans, recommending that they stay hidden during the day, but also not to worry because there were no spies in Cese.

"If you really want to go out during the day," Dad advised, "go into the woods where there are a lot of caves. They are very beautiful; put reeds in front of them and, if something happens, hide."

But they didn't know how to sort themselves out, they were a bit clumsy.

A few days later we agreed to share them out with some families from Cese, one for each. This decision was arrived at because five people were really too many to feed, especially just then.

Having agreed on this, we wondered how to divide up the prisoners. We wanted to avoid choosing because of the embarrassment it might cause. One of them was an exceptionally good young man who said to my mother: "I want to stay here. Here good."

"I would be happy with that," said my poor mother, "but how can we do it?"

In the end they drew lots and Albert came with us; he was the most cultured but at the same time the bossiest. He had wounds on his hands, but they weren't abrasions. They looked like little ulcers, perhaps because of the cold outside, and they continued to be red despite the medication that Mum had given to all of them. We had to ask the doctor for special medications to heal Albert's hands, and it was not easy: he had to have the pharmacist do it, in secret, but eventually he recovered.

The five prisoners were settled in, but there were about 20 families in Cese, perhaps more, so when other prisoners arrived they were sheltered in other houses. Some families also looked after two prisoners.

Normally they stayed the night in barns or abandoned houses. It was only when there was snow, and you could be sure that the fascists would not turn up, that they stayed in our houses.

Albert was very polite, a respectable person. He must have been 27 years old and he came from New York; he told us that his mother was Russian. He was fond of Mum and he said: "I love Mum because Mum is beautiful!"

I said: "Well, if Mum was ugly, wouldn't you still love her?"

"No!" he answered, but I never knew if he was joking or being serious.

Of course, they came from a more advanced country than ours, and so they viewed us with somewhat critical eyes, perhaps sardonic or perhaps, at times, deliberately teasing us.

But he was also protective of us. Once he said to me: "Diva, when you see us men laughing, don't laugh with us, because you don't know what we're talking about. You don't understand what we're saying, we are speaking English."

Well, he warned me.

When he arrived in the mornings, all cold, Mother made him hot toast with jam and he was always grateful.

But there were also moments of tension, such as when my father learned of the death of a friend of his, which occurred at Monte San Martino station. He had cycled just under our house, on his way to take the train for Amandola, and he was strafed by an Allied plane. When we heard the news, Dad cried. The next day Albert came to lunch and he began to say provocatively: "I heard important news, our planes have struck again, great, great."

Then Dad got angry and said: "Look, you are an imbecile!"

"I don't understand, Lorenzo," he replied, looking at him straight in the face.

"You understand very well!" Dad said. "You understand what I say. You're making fun of us and our feelings, but remember that if you were a German or a Pole or a fascist or Nazi I would still have done the same as we are doing for you. We do it out of compassion. You could have been anyone. We didn't shelter you because you are American, but because you are in need. Who do you think you are to mock our feelings?"

But Albert kept saying: "I don't understand. I don't understand!"

It was clear that things were getting heated because Albert knew what Dad was saying. But he stuck to his ironic tone until finally Dad said: "Do I have to force you to understand?" And he pointed at the shotgun hanging on the wall.

Like the rest of us, Dad was offended by Albert's behaviour. But Albert piped down and then, after lunch, he left. After that he never came to eat. Sometimes he passed by and said to Mum: "Better to eat polenta at a *contadino*'s house than to eat meat at Renzo's."

And he said to me: "*Signora*, your mum good, you good, but Lorenzo bad!"

"Dad's not bad," I said. "Why are you making fun of us?"

Even when we were dancing, when we were having parties, Albert mocked our movements, our dances, saying that there were beautiful dances in America. At that time, when we were singing, "*O Campagnola bella*" was doing the rounds. And he imitated our way of singing, changing the shape of our mouths, to mock us. One of the prisoners said that before the war he worked in a factory making nylon stockings, but we didn't even know what those things were at that time. Of course, we were a little more backward than them, but that was no justification for his attitude.

The other prisoners, who were cut from a different cloth, said that he was always provocative, even with them, and behaved like a bully.

One of them, Urbano, a practising Catholic, had a rosary chain around his neck and ended up in a family where they said the rosary every evening, and he participated very willingly.

And Bill? I remember he didn't learn any Italian words, he just said "*Vino bono!*" and he was always a little tipsy.

All of them joined in the work that the *contadini* did in the countryside, Albert was the only one who did not step up. Sometimes you'd see him when Dad was chopping wood, but he didn't like to get involved.

Although relations slowly mended, Albert always showed an equivocal attitude. Dad always advised him not to walk on the road, because it was dangerous: he might meet a German or a fascist. He suggested he go through the fields, taking shortcuts. And he always replied with that ironic tone of his: "No, if I meet German, I talk to him. My German friends, I go with them willingly."

After the winter the fascists and the Germans were seen more often and the risk of them capturing prisoners or partisans was really acute. One day a column of vehicles was seen arriving and a boy ran to sound the alarm, to warn the prisoners of the danger. As soon as they got out of the trucks the soldiers began to scatter like crazy people through the woods, where they met Zeno, a young local man. They immediately began to mistreat him, saying: "Where do you come from? Where are you going? Where are the prisoners?"

"I don't know. I don't know! I didn't see!" he replied, terrified.

So they beat him up – who knows how many blows they gave him – until they let him go, bruised all over. But he hadn't told, he didn't say where the prisoners were hidden.

However, the Nazis managed to capture seven or maybe eight prisoners. Towards evening you could hear them all coming back, pleased as punch, shooting in the air and singing. I thought they would kill them, and I was terrified, locked in the house with Mum. At one point we heard voices and looked out of the window: there were soldiers and prisoners drinking wine as if they were friends; they were drinking toasts with each other. One of the prisoners, who we knew well, looked up and caught our glance, shaking his head as if to say: "That's it, we've had it!" Meanwhile, a German said as he was drinking: "We all friends, all brothers."

A few days later Albert was taken too and went with the Germans, but I don't think he went voluntarily; they caught him just as he was walking along the road. Spring was at its height. A van full of Germans passed by, they saw him, stopped and a soldier asked for his papers. They took him away, along with other prisoners.

Albert came back after the war and told us that he had been deported to Germany and then to France. Anyway, thank God, he managed to survive. He often returned to Italy, even when our poor mother died, and every year was different: he came first with his wife, then with children. And more gifts, and many memories.

From a conversation with Diva Papiri (born 1925); Montefalcone Appennino, October 1999

Gino Leoni

How many of them will have died, poor souls!

I don't remember exactly when the prisoners escaped, perhaps a day or two after the initial confusion, but it definitely happened at night. There were lots of them, so many it was like a carnival, all running away. A few hundred metres away from the camp there was a bank with thick scrub, acacias all full of thorns, considered impenetrable, but the prisoners threw themselves in there in heaps, like a landslide, flattening it, and all this while the guards were shooting.

We knew about the prisoners at the concentration camp. We saw them when they went out of it, accompanied by armed guards, to go to the football field or to do physical training. We threw them bundles of vine prunings, they took the most tender twigs and broke them into small pieces to make tea. They always waved at us and thanked us. I lived a few hundred metres from the camp, in front of the cemetery, and I often heard the prisoners talking or singing. One of them, called Manuel Serrano, I met some time later because he came to live in Servigliano. We also knew of an escape tunnel dug by the prisoners; it was said to be hundreds of metres long, but this was just rumour.

When the escape took place we heard gunfire from our house and some people must have been killed. The fascists were certainly firing. A Greek from Cyprus screamed in agony all night, and only the day after was he taken to the cemetery.

Two other Cypriots asked for help at our house a few days after the escape. All the prisoners were looking for a refuge to save their lives, scattering and hiding from the fascists who were shooting, trying to recapture them. There were five of us at home: Dad, Mum, Marino, my sister and I; the other two were away at the war. Despite the problems, we hid them in the stable where the beasts were kept. They showed up during the day, and when she saw them my poor mother immediately thought of my brothers, prisoners of the British and the Americans, and from whom we had had no news. Two men, who spoke a bit of Italian, asked for help. They were young, tall and strong and Mother told us to prepare a hiding place behind the hay in the stable, and they stayed there for eight days. They would get out through a hole and they relieved themselves in the stable. They stayed hidden all the time, day and night. Several times, when fascists appeared outside the house looking for prisoners, they were inside keeping silent, next to the animals.

We were very careful and brought them food at the animals' feeding time so as not to arouse suspicion; there were eight cows and some sheep. Unfortunately there was no opportunity to talk quietly with them and we managed to find out very little. I don't even remember their names.

One day, when we took food to them, they told us that they were going to leave because they were too close to the village and the risk was too great; they would try to reach the Americans towards the south. They thanked us and we saw them heading for the fields. We never heard any more of them.

Anyway, travelling only on foot, through fields and scrubland, who knows if they managed to reach Allied lines. How many of them will have died, poor souls! Fascists lurked near the passes to shoot any prisoners who were trying to get away through the scrub by the river.

The Germans did come by to search the house, luckily just a few days after the prisoners had left. We were renting and the landlord had kept for himself a large basement for all his valuables, the door being closed with a padlock. After searching the house they also asked to see the locked basement. Our explanation – that it did not belong to us, that the boss had the key – was in vain, for they forced the lock with an iron bar and opened the door. They looked around and left.

The Germans could do so much harm to the population but, all in all, they did not perform acts of serious brutality, despite the attacks they suffered at Parapina and Servigliano, where a number of their soldiers were killed. The American bombing – what with the dead, the wounded and the destruction – caused more damage than the Germans. So many tears!

However, it was really the fascists who engendered fear, who were shooting, who threatened us. How many times did we have to endure it! We always had to show our ration card, but even then they didn't give you what was due to you and, if you protested, you could lose the right to another card. They were all in cahoots, the fascists and the shopkeepers. One year they didn't want us to thresh the wheat. We waited for days and risked losing everything. So Dad grabbed the pitchfork and, looking straight in the face of a fascist leader and his companions, ordered the owner of the thresher, Peppe Mercuri, to start the tractor and to start working, threatening: "If anyone comes near, I will stab him!"

That is how we managed to thresh the corn that was piled up in front of the house, and, after we had done it, others followed suit.

When the Germans withdrew they opened the grain silos in all the villages, taking away what they could and leaving everyone the chance to collect supplies. They even went into the camp after the prisoners had escaped, to get blankets and other things, but someone starting shooting and two people were killed.

Nowadays it's hard to talk about these things. No-one listening has any idea, the children tell us we were idiots because we sold a ton of wheat to get two of maize and we ate polenta instead of bread, but it was the only way to survive. These days no-one can understand such things.

But I do not look forward to the future: what a waste! We will definitely pay for all of this, sad to say.

From a conversation with Gino Leoni (born 1922); Servigliano, October 1999

Neno Brugnolini

He let off a shot unintentionally

Neno Brugnolini

On 8 September 1943 I was in Rome, at Tiburtina. The king had run away with Badoglio and we were abandoned! I was in the air force and was part of a detachment of the Third Air Squadron, near Tiburtina station. The news of the Armistice was announced in the evening, around five o'clock, or maybe seven or eight, I don't remember exactly. That day I went to see my uncle, Giovanni, a colonel who worked in the War Department. We all thought with relief that the war was over and when I returned to the barracks we were absolutely euphoric. But a day later, on 9 September, there were no clear instructions, the officers did not know what to do and they were continuously ringing the switchboard of the Air

Ministry, where no-one answered. There was an increasing sense of anxiety among us soldiers, and it was impossible to fully understand the situation.

On 10 September Germans from Frascati entered Porta San Paolo and occupied Rome. There were still no orders for us soldiers and we had nothing, not even a handgun, to defend ourselves with: we had been abandoned by everyone. Mussolini was with the Germans and the king and Badoglio had fled from Rome. With no orders, with no-one to tell us what to do, everyone began to run away. I too left Tiburtina, on foot, and managed to get to Monterotondo station. I was still in uniform but I also wore mechanic's overalls, because I was an aeroplane mechanic.

Night had fallen. There were many comrades with me but no-one knew how to get back home. Then we heard an announcement on the station loudspeaker that soldiers were permitted to take the train to Ancona. I thought that if I could reach Ancona I could get close to home.

So, I took the train too!

We realised immediately that it was a German trap to capture us, to arrest the soldiers who were no longer under command and who had spread out over the area. They did not permit us to get out of the wagons and, after a long journey, the next morning we arrived in Ancona. At the station the Germans surrounded the train with the intention of arresting all of us.

Luckily, however, I still managed to escape. These days I'm slow, but back then I was quick and, in a trice, I jumped off the train and tried my luck in the direction of an Italian railway shed, where there was a lathe for the engine wheels.

The Germans must have noticed that I had escaped because they came back with machine guns. Meanwhile, other people had also tried to escape like me and I heard shots and screams.

I was wearing air force mechanic overalls and I immediately removed the epaulettes and sat down on top of the lathe. I heard the Germans coming closer and closer, so I put a hand into the bogie that was full of oil and I made myself dirty all over, to make it look as if I was working there. A moment later the soldiers came in with machine guns, accompanied by two Carabinieri. One of the Germans slowly advanced towards me, pointing the gun barrel in my direction and lifting metal sheets to find me, while the other said *"kaput, kaput!"* He wanted to kill me. However, the two policemen who were with them, even though they no longer had any control over anything and had to obey only the Germans, saw that I was sitting on the lathe. Mistaking me for a worker, they made gestures to signify that I was not the fugitive and they went on their way.

Outside the shed two railway workers were watching this scene and they almost cried when they saw the state I was in. Finally, having checked around a bit, the Germans decided to leave and ignored me.

The railway workers immediately came up to me and said: "It's incredible! How did you manage to get away with that?"

"I have no idea!" I replied in a daze.

"Where are you from?"

"From Le Marche, from Servigliano near Fermo. If I can't take a train to Porto San Giorgio, I will try to walk home!" I had decided.

"Look, there's a train going to Pescara now," they said, lowering their voices. "It is a goods train."

I hadn't touched food for 24 hours and suddenly I was overcome with hunger pangs. I asked how I could catch this train and was told it was made up of a lot of wagons for animal transportation and that it came from Gorizia.

They added: "If you want to get on, we'll leave a door open for you in a livestock wagon, and as soon as the train is moving you can jump in and get away. But be careful: if the Germans see you, they will kill you."

The train was headed to Pescara to take on airport equipment and was manned by the Germans, but the two railwaymen were not aware of this important detail.

As soon as the train moved off they whistled to tell me to run, and I jumped into the wagon. I didn't have time to catch my breath before seeing that there were other men in there too: they were five policemen from Gorizia, carrying haversacks full of hand grenades and armed to the teeth. But they told me that they too had run away, that they were from Abruzzo and were trying to make for home.

They were so tense that they almost wanted to throw me off the train: "Where are you going you coward, scoundrel? Can't you see that we're here, do you want us to be discovered?"

They had covered the windows with their coats to prevent the Germans from spotting them. I kept quiet as the train rolled along and after we had gone through the tunnel past Ancona we arrived at Osimo station.

I thought to myself: "Well, here I am. It's better if I get off and go to Loreto to my relative who is a monk, maybe he can help me."

As soon as the train stopped we saw a lot of Germans. Cautiously I opened the door and saw that they were uncoupling the wagons to load some supplies, perhaps from Loreto airport. In an instant I jumped down from the wagon door, but I didn't notice the German who was opening the doors on the other side to carry out checks.

I waited there, petrified, while he was looking into the darkness of the wagon. I heard the five Carabinieri moving about, as if they were loading a weapon. This was also noticed by the German, who became alarmed and immediately began to blow his whistle to summon assistance. At the same time he must have noticed me and called "Halt!" and then, opening the door wider, saw the armed Carabinieri.

A few seconds later, two more Germans arrived, climbed into the wagons and shouted *"Raus, Raus,"* ("Out, Out"), forcing the Carabinieri out of the wagon while I was still stuck outside. They took us over to the wall of the station. There were six of us, but I was not armed; one German pointed a machine gun at our chests while the other two disarmed the Carabinieri, forcing them to drop their trousers. I was looking at all this, staring at the Germans in the eye because, being near the corner of the wall, I was waiting for a good time to escape. As soon as I saw I was not being observed I carefully went round the corner and began to run past the station and ended up across the street, in a grocery store. There was a woman there with a little girl by her side who was watching everything. The woman told me to go into a basement under the stairs and to arrange some dried salt cod barrels to hide behind.

"Where are you from?" she asked me.

"I'm from Servigliano. The Germans are after me, I've been on the road a long time."

"Quiet, for goodness' sake! They'll kill those poor people! They have guns pointed at their chests."

"I was with them."

"Yes. Yes. I saw everything," she said anxiously.

"Are you hungry?"

"I haven't eaten anything for a long time," I replied.

She gave me a jar of jam that I devoured without bread, because there wasn't any left.

Watching me, the little girl exclaimed: "Oh Mother, that soldier is so hungry!"

"Be quiet, girl, remember your father is in Russia and we have had no news for a year," the woman burst into tears.

I was hiding behind the dried-fish barrels and was observing all of this.

In the meantime the Germans had realised that I had escaped and, out of spite, had decided to deport the stationmaster to Germany. After the Germans had left with the prisoners this was reported to me, actually by the stationmaster himself, who told me everything, including that it was only at the last minute that he convinced them to let him go.

Then he added: "Where do you live? Where are you headed?"

"Porto San Giorgio," I replied. "Oh, if I could get there I could walk home from there."

He told me that in a little while another train, completely uncovered, would leave Osimo bound for Pescara.

"Have a word with the train drivers and see if they can slow down to let you jump off at Porto San Giorgio."

I went up and talked to the drivers, who were very alarmed by the constant threats from the Germans. But they told me that they would reduce speed at Porto San Giorgio to let me get off.

Their kindness was such that, because it was dark, they even stopped the train a short way outside the station to allow me to jump off without running the risk of falling or meeting Germans. Next to the railway track it was pitch dark, you couldn't see a thing, and I hid in a ravine until the morning. At first light, moving very cautiously to avoid mishaps, I took the little train to Amandola and I managed to get to Servigliano and then home.

I survived by a whisker and, if I think of those poor comrades, dead or deported, I wonder how it had been possible.

When I arrived, the Servigliano concentration camp had already been opened up and everyone had left: the prisoners had escaped and gone into hiding with local families and the soldiers had returned home.

Only the Carabinieri and the marshal were still there; the latter had apparently mistreated the prisoners and, when the Allies arrived, an American ex-prisoner arrested him.

When I got home the Santa Lucia district was full of prisoners who were in hiding and receiving assistance from families. Everyone was fond of them. There were British prisoners, Poles, Americans, Russians: even Russia was represented here. The *contadini* gave them clothes and fed them, but secretly, to avoid searches and reprisals by fascists and Nazis. Even so, some families had their houses burned down for giving aid to prisoners, nearby, along the river Ete.

We didn't have any prisoners in my house because we were too close to the road, but we gave them lots of stuff to eat and to clothe themselves. I remember Jack and John who often came to eat with us.

I too had to go into hiding, because Mussolini had recalled everyone to arms, but I did not appear.

Everything went well with the prisoners, we were like brothers.

Well, there was one case of a Greek Cypriot called Paris, who was with a local family. He spoke Italian better than we did and had been welcomed into that house like a son; in fact they had given him the clothes of their actual son who was a prisoner in England and they treated him like a lord.

He used to walk past my house a lot and we'd chat about this and that.

To cut a long story short, no-one ever really knew the reason, perhaps it was because of a love affair with a girl of the house; anyway, Paris must have fallen out with her father, whose name was Giulio. One morning, when the Germans were preparing to leave Servigliano, Paris was holding an Italian musket, a .38 and, perhaps unintentionally, let off a shot that bounced off the door frame of the stable and hit poor Giulio, perforating his abdomen.

We are talking about an accident, certainly he did not mean to shoot to kill. In fact he did not shoot facing him, but the shot must have gone off by accident and, when it hit the iron door frame, the bullet shattered and one splinter hit our neighbour.

I don't really know what happened after this shooting, because I was in hiding and I could not go anywhere, but a lot of people went to offer help, all in vain. The poor man hung on in agony for a few days but didn't have medical help and eventually he died. Paris, on the other hand, fled after the accident and nothing more was heard of him. Of course, no-one ever knew where he got the weapon from; some said he got it from the "patriots", others had different opinions. In any case, there was no news of Paris after the accident.

There were two English prisoners, Jack and John, the latter housed with the teacher Pia, who came to serious blows in the cantina in Curetta because one said that they were now the masters, since Italy had lost the war, while the other objected that our families, all of the people, treated them as if they were sons and brothers. This took place in the winter. It was cold and there were lots of people in the cellar, and the two of them were covered with blood. It wasn't easy to prise them apart. It was scary.

With the Germans still out there, the two of them were fighting because one of them felt like the conqueror and the other one was showing gratitude, saying: "The families give us clothes, they feed us and they even give us beds to sleep in. They are risking their own lives, how can you talk like that?"

When the Americans arrived, all the prisoners presented themselves at their headquarters to be signed in and to give an account of how they had managed to survive for almost a year. Then the Americans decided to make awards to those families who had suffered damage as a result of their generosity; for instance, for that house burned by the Germans near the river Ete. Almost all of them received gifts.

They gave Marino of Bardò an American Jeep; they gave the Poles, who had their command post at Casa Monti in Servigliano, petrol and oil to thresh the wheat.

How much hardship we had suffered to achieve our freedom! Of course, in any struggle for freedom there are those who commit dastardly acts, but the fight against fascism "caused rivers of tears".

From a conversation with Neno Brugnolini (born 1925); Servigliano, July 2000

Giovanni Pilotti

I still receive greetings

I was born in America and I moved to Italy in the 1930s with my parents. Here I did middle school, high school and then university. We had returned to Italy because Mum was not very well; the doctors we had consulted said that perhaps she would benefit from being in her home country and her nervous disorders could be healed. Mum was very homesick for her country and family, my grandmother and uncles who had stayed there. I had been in Italy since I was about six years old; my sister was born in America and there was a four-year difference between me and her, she was younger than me.

When we arrived in Italy my parents wondered what to have me do, so they decided to register me for middle school. This was during the fascist era.

When war broke out we moved to the countryside on the slope of the Penna area that borders the Salino river, near woods, on the estate that once upon a time belonged to the Counts Colucci. Using the money my father had sent him from America, my grandfather had bought a "hunting lodge" with a few hectares of land, about 40, and we settled there. The plot of land was like a ship whose bow bordered thermal baths. Of course, as a student I lived away from home, between Macerata and Fermo. More precisely, I was a student at the high school in Macerata and in the final year I went to school in Fermo. Then I enrolled at the University of Medicine in Perugia, after which I went to Bologna for my last year.

I always liked a change of scenery, and in the senior year I changed a lot.

When Badoglio signed the Armistice with the Americans I was about 20 years old and I was in Penna San Giovanni. I remember that on 8 September there was a great to-do that also affected me in a way. I had been called up but when I went for my medical I was deferred to the following year because of a weak constitution, perhaps because I was extremely thin. So I managed not to respond to the call to arms that the Italian Social Republic had announced at that time.

The year after, I was asked to report to the Military District and I was declared fit for service, so I went into hiding.

My father had even constructed a cave down in the woods, but I never went there. You know, at that age you don't think very much about the risks you are running.

As I was saying, after 8 September 1943 the prisoners appeared. Most of them were from Servigliano, but there were also some from Sforzacosta, where there was another prison camp. That camp had been planned to accommodate prisoners mainly from Britain, Australia and New Zealand, whereas Servigliano was mainly intended for Americans. But there were also a lot of British prisoners there too.

When the first prisoners appeared, my Mum was on a piece of land that we had on the Tennacola and she immediately realised who they were. Of course, they began to speak in English, a language that she knew very well and this meant she could understand what they needed.

My father also went right away to show them where they could settle, in the abandoned house of a *contadino* who had emigrated to America. These were the first three prisoners, all of them Americans. I remember perfectly the surname of one of them – Poleri – because I started corresponding with him at the end of the war and even went to stay with him in Philadelphia in America. He was an Italian American of Sicilian origin. Then there were the other two: James was one, but I don't remember the name of the other.

After these three, others arrived in the area too and we settled all of them as best we could. We had a radio in our house and many of them came to listen to it because we could receive Radio London (London Calling Europe) and the English stations.

Over the course of a few days they had become a large group and they lived off whatever the peasants, showing great selflessness, could offer them.

The prisoners lived in out-of-the-way abandoned houses, away from the roads, maybe hidden in the woods, but they had beds, blankets, clothes and all the essentials for living, of course provided by the *contadini*. I went to visit them often, since I could speak English and could communicate with them easily. They didn't do any real work, but they got organised and made themselves useful, carrying out any chore that allowed them to express their gratitude and to occupy their time. On these occasions, staying on to eat at the house, they strengthened the ties of friendship.

When the influx of soldiers was at its height I think I am right in saying that there were five or six hundred prisoners who survived thanks to the generosity of the *contadini*; almost every house in Penna helped at least one. If I reflect on it, I am moved by the solidarity shown towards those poor people. And it wasn't just a question of feeding them; it was also about establishing human relationships and friendships.

There were many of them – scattered across the area covering Penna, Gualdo and Sarnano – and they kept in contact with each other. One of them, who was from New York and whom I liked a lot, decided to leave. It was winter, that cold winter of 1943, and at night I often took him with me to the village, to meet the families. This type of movement always took place in the dark because the Carabinieri were vigilant and the fascists were even more dangerous.

In fact one day the Carabinieri came to my house to seal up the radio, because they had heard that we had been listening to Radio London. My mother tried to justify it, saying that, because I was in the last year of high school and lived in Fermo all week, when I came home I enjoyed listening and changing stations. Without adding that the house could be full of British and American ex-prisoners who, as well as listening to the radio, sat round the fire talking and drinking a glass of wine! It was Mother who, three or four days later, broke the seals and decided to switch on the radio.

I was mentioning that American prisoner, whose name was Martin Deutsch; he was of German origin but Jewish by religion. He confided to me that he was engaged in America to a girl of Italian extraction; contrary to our advice, he decided to leave. We had suggested that he should wait because in a few weeks we expected an attack by the Allies, who were on the Pescara line. However, he left from Penna with another ex-prisoner, a former policeman from Boston. They managed to reach Porto San Giorgio or San Benedetto del Tronto, and they sailed from there on Allied ships.

Some time later, during my trip to America, I did some research with the US authorities and I learned that Martin and his comrade had both died during a naval battle in the Channel and they were buried in Belgium.

I also remember Manuel Serrano, who was a tall, nice, exuberant Puerto Rican; he sometimes passed through the Penna countryside and he knew a lot of people.

Before the liberation the situation had become highly critical for everyone. I had to go on the run too because the marshal of the Carabinieri, a man from Abruzzo, who was disinclined to show blind obedience to fascist instructions, had warned my mother that they should get me away and that one should be careful with the prisoners. He had heard that there was about to be a round-up by the Nazi-Fascists. So Father asked some relatives who lived in Magliano di Terrato to hide me for a while and recommended that I walk there, using smaller paths to avoid being detected. However, after I had packed my suitcase I set off with a defiant air towards La Parapina through which the old railway passed. I took the train from there and alighted at Magliano without any difficulty, pleased with myself and my courage. I stayed with those relatives for a fortnight and then, when the state of alert had subsided, I returned to Penna.

Once home I learned that there had been round-ups and that, during one of these, a Republican had shot an Englishman. The prisoner died almost immediately from his injuries at the hospital in Penna and was buried in the town cemetery. It was not until the war had ended that his body was exhumed and transported home. Fortunately, there were no reprisals against the families that had housed the prisoners, also because the searches had not revealed anything.

After the Liberation I felt the need to thank the marshal of the Carabinieri and I abstained from joining in retaliation against the people in Penna who were known to be fascists. When a British patrol of about a dozen servicemen arrived from Porto San Giorgio, carrying a list of people held responsible for fascist violence according to reports from Allied prisoners, they sought me out for help. Well, I decided to let bygones be bygones and protect them all, saying that they were fascists in name but had never done anything wrong. There was only one I did not defend – a primary school teacher – because I had found out that he had reported the prisoners' movements to the Carabinieri, putting every family at risk. He was taken to Fermo prison and was released after a few months.

After the war many relationships were kept alive by means of letters and visits. I know that one of the men from my area even found work in America through an ex-prisoner who had been sheltered in his house. I corresponded with some of them and had the opportunity to visit them during my travels in America. I still get Christmas greetings from some of my friends across the ocean.

From a conversation with Giovanni Pilotti (born 1923); Penna San Giovanni, 23 January 2001

Superio Marinangeli

Let's hope he forgot about us

That September everything was changing.

A lot of prisoners who had escaped from the concentration camps were roaming around the countryside. One of them turned up at our house. His name was Eddy and he was one of those who had fled from the camp at Sforzacosta in Macerata province.

We looked after him at home because he was in a really awful state. Despite the fact there were so many on the run, a lot of them did manage to find refuge in local houses. However, the Germans quickly re-arrested some of them when they carried out their shakedowns.

Truth to tell, not everyone in the area was generous to the prisoners, perhaps for fear of reprisals or perhaps because our houses were searched frequently. One day German soldiers turned up at our house to ask if there were any prisoners, but we said no.

"Sure?" said the officer, in broken Italian.

"Absolutely sure!" my mother answered.

We had known about the impending search because from the top of the village we could see trucks advancing towards us and we passed on the word immediately. A moment later the prisoners vanished from the houses and hid in gullies, in areas of scrub or in barns.

Eddy stayed with us for many months, maybe six or seven. Of course, my father took precautions to prevent fascists or Germans finding out that he was in the house.

He advised Eddy: "There is no problem with you eating here, but during the day you must stay hidden."

And Eddy replied: "Yes, yes!"

Then Mother murmured: "But where can he go . . . it's dangerous . . . it is best that he doesn't go too far away."

Eventually my father decided to put him in the hayloft near the house. The hay was stacked high and he used a ladder to get up to it; moreover, in the case of danger, it could also be an excellent hiding place.

Sometimes Eddy moved from his hiding place to visit other prisoners who had been housed in the countryside around us. On occasions they even arranged to meet at the local shop.

He didn't do much work, partly because it was dangerous to do so.

We had a good relationship with him: he was always very well-mannered. You could see he was a responsible person. He expressed his gratitude and said: "You are risking a lot for me."

Throughout the winter he sat with us every evening in front of the hearth, and after a while he asked my brother if he could have some bread for toasting in the embers, because he loved that. All you had to do was add a drop of oil and a pinch of salt and he was happy. Sometimes he would sidle up to Dad and say: "Dad, a little drop of wine?"

And Dad always indulged him, smiling.

He was like a person who belonged there. We always gave him the same food as we were eating.

I remember we made bread every week and, since we also had laying hens, we even made ring cakes. This was the sweet that accompanied our coffee, which was made of barley, of course.

My brother often went to Fermo because he was studying there. One day he told us that he had discovered there was a chance for the prisoners to get a boat on which they could sail to Pescara to join up with the Allies.

So Eddy started to think about this with his mates. He wanted to leave to try and reach the Front.

One day he went to Macerata with some of his friends and, when he came home, he brought three beautiful pieces of fabric. He said: "I don't know when your birthday is, but it can't be far away and this is for you. It's just a little something."

My mother became alarmed and immediately asked him where they had got hold of that material.

"It was given to us by a friend near Macerata," Eddy replied.

The next night he promised that he would write to us and then he left with his friends.

We never heard a word from him again!

When they left, the only information they had was that they could get a boat near Pedaso. We don't know if he's dead or if he's forgotten about us. Let's hope he's forgotten about us.

From a conversation with Superio Marinangeli (born 1922); Monte Vidon Corrado, March 2001

Licinio Licini

She made Billy dress as a woman

Licinio Licini

I was a boy at the time of the Armistice. I recall those days perfectly because the facts of which I speak are imprinted on my memory.

Thanks to my mother, who was an elementary school teacher, we were pretty well informed on what was happening. As soon as the news of the Armistice got out there was an explosion of joy because we were convinced the war would be over. At home we were all happy and our thoughts turned to a cousin, a prisoner in Africa, who it was hoped would return soon. Instead, things didn't go as everybody expected.

It was then that Billy turned up. He had escaped, along with three others (all British) from the prisoner of war camp at Sforzacosta, by digging a hole under the gates. As the guards realised immediately that they had escaped, as soon as the men reached the Fiastra river they threw themselves into the water and hid themselves, breathing through reeds. Some hours later, realising that things had quietened down, they set off in a southerly direction. They were soaking wet but they succeeded in reaching Loro Piceno, where a family took them in. They were fed but were then asked to move on.

Walking across fields the men arrived at Montappone, where the Selva family looked after them for a few days. But it was dangerous there too, so the men had to press on. After a few kilometres they again found a welcome, this time from the Ciccale family of Montevidone, not far from here. Word of their presence quickly got around the neighbourhood and, to avoid the burden falling solely on one family, many others took turns to feed them. So, one time they would come to our house, on another they would go to one of our neighbours.

One day my mother got summoned by a *contadino*, Umberto Marzialetti, because one of the prisoners had fallen ill. My mother's name was Brunilde Polidori. As a teacher and as an educated person she was considered capable of understanding what was wrong with him and how he might be cured. She immediately went to our neighbours, along with me. As soon as we got there we found the prisoner slumped on a chair, complaining of a headache and a high temperature. Realising the situation was serious, my mother said: "Umberto, he is not well. I'll take him to my house. I have sons and I'm aware that in life one can never know what's going to happen."

So we took him home. My mother placed him in my bed, in the room I shared with my brother, while I had to sleep with my parents. "So, if the Germans or fascists come looking for him, we can say that it is you who is in the bed," she told me.

The house was large but there were eight of us, comprising my family and that of my uncle. Two families but essentially a single one: we did everything together.

We immediately became friends: we were like brothers. Billy spoke a little Italian and was always polite. Of course, we were worried, also because we heard of some family who, having given aid to the prisoners, had suffered violence from the Germans and fascists. But we were very careful. Billy hardly ever left the house; at most he would go outside and immediately slip into the stable where we had a horse. My father had property and used the horse to get around.

Straightaway we made Billy change as he was wearing military uniform. My mother gave him clothes that had belonged to an uncle who had recently died. He lacked nothing, except perhaps for cigarettes because he was a big smoker. To keep him happy my father got hold of tobacco leaves which Billy used to roll cigarettes, but they weren't very good. Luckily the British authorities got to hear that there were prisoners in the area who were short of clothes and other things. One night there was a parachute drop containing civilian clothes, shoes and lots of other stuff, above all cigarettes. When he got to hear about this Billy told his comrades that he wouldn't take anything as he lacked for nothing, but that he wanted the cigarettes. And that's what happened.

One day my mother invited a young man, originally from Puglia, who was staying with friends of ours, because it was said he spoke English well. We didn't know much about him: some said that he had fled from the fascists, just vague rumours. Anyway, the young man came and talked with Billy for some hours. A few days later we heard that the young man, whom I won't name, had disappeared and enlisted with the fascists. My mother immediately began to fear the worst, thinking that he might denounce us.

One morning, while we were at the gate about to go out on to the road and head for school, my mother saw a lorry load of Germans approach, on their way from Montevidone to Montappone. As the road wasn't asphalted but was a narrow grass track, we stopped in front of the gate and Mum said: "We'll let them pass and then carry on."

Instead, as soon as the lorry arrived in front of our house it stopped right at the gate, blocking our route. Immediately some soldiers jumped down and one of them took my mother by the arm and said confidently, in broken Italian: "Mother, you have an Englishman in this house named Billy!"

It was early morning. Dad was in the stable and Billy was sleeping peacefully in my room. My mother was in shock. The German soldier repeated: "Mother, there is an Englishman here named Billy, he has tattoos on his body, hasn't he?"

"No!" she replied, in desperation. "Somebody we can rely on gave us this information," continued the soldier.

"That might be so but I know nothing," Mum repeated.

Meanwhile she was wondering how to warn Billy, who was certainly still asleep. It was a terrible moment. Luckily the noise of the lorry had alerted my aunt who just then was leaning out of the window.

"Viviana, Viviana," my mother yelled at her, "these soldiers say there is an Englishman in our house."

"But that's not true!" exclaimed my aunt.

Then she went back inside and hurried towards the entrance. As soon as she got outside she shut the door behind her.

In the meantime the soldiers had climbed down from the lorry and were surrounding the house, also blocking my father who was in the stable. Dad asked what was going on but nobody replied because only the officer who was with us spoke Italian.

Some of the Germans went up to my aunt and the officer told her that they wanted to check the house at once.

My aunt took them to the ground floor, which contained the cellar and other rooms that served for stores. Just then my mother entered the house, hastened to the first floor and softly began to call out: "Billy, Billy."

"Yes, Mum," he replied.

Billy swiftly realised what was happening and hurried behind Mum, who gestured to him to follow her. We had a trap door in the slabs on the first floor that led to a storeroom dug out between two walls of the ground floor. It was a way of hiding the corn and other farm produce that we were obliged to hand over to the authorities. The trap door was hidden by an old chest full of books and magazines. It was really heavy to move but, when occasion demanded, it could be moved because on one side it was supported by a baton that served as a roller. It was a secret hideaway because at that time everybody came to ask questions, on occasions even forcibly. There were Germans, fascists and even partisans.

The trap door was narrow and was kept closed by one of those big brick slabs that the floor was made of. While the soldiers checked the ground floor my mother, with help from Billy, shifted the chest and opened up the trap door. With some difficulty and considerably flustered, as one can imagine, Billy slipped into the storeroom. Hearing the Germans talk at the bottom of the stairs, Mum quickly put back the slab and began to move the chest to cover everything up.

Suddenly, while she was rotating the chest, which weighed at least 200 kilos, the baton serving as a roller slipped out, leaving the slab exposed. Those magazines belonged to Mum, who adored reading, but right then she despaired for her favourite pastime. Meanwhile the Germans were starting to come up the stairs and Mum still had that chest to put back into place. With an effort born of desperation she lifted it on one side and shoved it towards the wall. Not even she could explain how she found the strength required but, in the course of a single week, she shed 10 kilos.

In the meantime the soldiers had reached the first floor, but my aunt shrewdly directed them towards the bedroom where her husband, my uncle, slept. He was bedridden due to an accident at work.

"Please don't go in with your guns in hand because my husband's not well and he might get alarmed," she begged.

Rather reluctantly the soldiers did as she asked. They went into the room and searched everywhere: under the bed, in the wardrobe, in the chest, naturally without finding anything.

As this was going on the German who spoke Italian began to shout: "Mr Billy, we know you're here. Come out before something happens."

Billy didn't move, of course.

There was another room on the first floor that we used as a storeroom and the soldiers stopped there to look it over. My mother silently joined the group and, once inside the storeroom, she invited the soldiers to take the grapes that we had hung between the beams to dry out.

"No thank you, *Signora*," replied the German. "Our rules don't permit that."

Finding nothing, they carried on searching the other rooms in the house.

A few seconds before the Germans entered my bedroom my brother, who was wide awake but who had not yet got up, noticed that Billy, in his hurry, had left his wallet on the bedside cabinet. In desperation he quickly jumped up, slipped the wallet inside his pyjamas and got back into bed.

The soldiers had a look around but found nothing. Eventually, after the soldiers had had a discussion, the one who spoke Italian went up to Mum and told her: "Mother, we're going but we are sure that there's an Englishman named Billy here."

"But there isn't," my mother insisted. "Where could we hide him? There isn't anywhere! Where would we put him at this hour of the morning? Lots of people come here and we give something to everybody but there's nobody in our house!"

Luckily they decided to go away. It had taken about an hour, but what an hour!

When we were left on our own my aunt realised that my father hadn't come out of the stable and she went to have a look: he was sitting on a log. My mother was shocked and exhausted. My brother too, who was already at university, had been shaken. Me too, being the youngest.

So as not to attract attention my mother and I went to school. When we got to the village we saw that everybody was alarmed by what had happened, because they knew that Billy was at our house.

"What's happened, have they found Billy?" asked the worried villagers.

"Billy? Billy left last week," my mother said.

"And where has he gone?"

"To the partisans in the mountains, I think."

"That's lucky," people commented.

Meanwhile Billy had come out of the storeroom bathed in sweat, but things were by no means safe – neither for him nor for us. So he decided to distance himself and went secretly to an abandoned house in the undergrowth at the gully, where he stayed for half a day or so.

That afternoon my mother returned to the village to confide in my grandmother and ask advice, because Billy certainly couldn't stay at our house. Nor, however, could we abandon him: he was one of us by now, one of the family. At grandmother's house there was also a woman who helped with jobs. Mum hesitated to talk in front of her but grandmother told her: "You can tell me everything freely because Rosina is part of the family now."

So Mum opened up and told the whole story. While they considered what to do, an amazing solution presented itself. Rosina, who lived in the village with two grandchildren in a house right next to the square, proposed that she should host the prisoner.

Then Mum said: "Don't worry about food because we'll bring everything needed. With the excuse of taking it to my mother I'll also bring some for Billy."

"However, I can't let him sleep in the bedrooms below because my granddaughters are still young," said Rosina thoughtfully. "That means that we'll make a room for him in the attic, a sort of canopy," she decided.

In the evening, to get Billy to this lady in the village, my mother resorted to a disguise: she made him dress as a woman, using her aunt's clothes. At that time there was no-one around in the streets anyway, and with a handkerchief around his head he was unrecognisable. They went out together, Billy and Mum, like two ladies, and they managed to reach the house of grandmother's maid without any problem.

Billy stayed there for three months, up to the arrival of the Americans. During the day he remained in the building, drawing or reading; in the evening he was with the family but as soon as he heard voices he immediately hid.

We didn't go to that house and couldn't start doing so in order not to attract attention. Therefore, when we went to church, as we left after Mass, glancing up we saw Billy's fingers waving at us through the gaps of the curtain blinds. Only Mum used to go, always giving us his news and passing on ours.

That winter Professor Carlo Costanzi, director of the Polyclinic at Rome, turned up in the village. He had brought his wife and daughters there so that they could stay somewhere safer. He often used to travel to Rome and knew people in the Vatican. So, thanks to him, we managed to get a letter from Billy to reach his family in England and receive a reply.

These were difficult days, during which blood was spilt between fascists and partisans, and tension was high. During one of these clashes a fascist chief was shot dead, a bank manager who lived at Montappone. The pervading atmosphere of vendetta was predictable.

In spring, as Easter approached, when my mother went to find Billy he constantly said: "Mum, Mum, take me home for Easter." He called my mother "Mum" because he said that his own mother had given birth to him but that she herself had given him back his life.

"How do we do that? It's dangerous," she said anxiously. Thinking it over, eventually Mum decided to get him to our house for Easter.

She said: "When the evening Mass on Saturday finishes, be ready, dressed as a woman. Go out of the main door and, mixing among the people, take the short cut and go directly to our house. And let's hope that God sends you safely." And that's what happened.

When he reached our house, in tears he kissed everybody. He took me in his arms and called me "my brother". There was great joy, as if a dear relative had come back.

My mother said tearfully: "Billy, it's just for tonight. Tomorrow you go back to Rosina's because it's too dangerous." She added: "Listen, the door must always stay shut."

Instead, we don't know how, the door remained open and a neighbour, a close friend of ours, came in. As soon as she climbed the stairs she saw Billy. Thinking he had been caught, he began to cry, he was so worried that something could happen.

"Hello Billy," she greeted him, "but why are you crying?"

"Because you've spotted me," he replied. "And now everybody will get to hear that I'm at the Licini's."

"I won't tell anybody anything," she assured him.

My mother also entreated her. "Brunilde, don't worry. I've said that I won't say a word to anybody and that's how it will be. Not even my husband will know!"

We spent the eve of Easter and Easter Day joyfully together. Then, as it grew dark, Billy went back to the village.

When the Allies arrived the word went round that the soldiers who had been looked after by families should report to military headquarters at Fermo. Billy went there but returned, saying that he wished to stay here; that this was now his family. My mother said firmly: "Your mother is expecting you and is certainly worrying about you. We are friends and our house is always open when you wish to come, but your duty is to go back home!"

And so it was: he was convinced and he went to Fermo.

Some days later we saw him back here again. We knew that when he returned to headquarters he was detained for punishment because he had absconded without permission.

Then he went to Naples and from there, too, he slipped away to our home for a few days. He had become too attached to us. But following that escape the military put him in clink to punish him, as if he were a deserter.

When he got back to England he wrote to both my mother and sisters. He was Welsh, from Newport, a Catholic.

My daughter went to find him during a visit to England. Then he moved to Canada and visits became more difficult, but he still telephones us and is always writing, repeating in Italian: "If I get to 80 years old, I owe it all to you."

At home after the war we often spoke about what had happened, of the danger we had run. But my mother insisted: "We had to do that, because life goes on. One day we give and another day we receive."

In 1945 the British, in recognition of those who had sheltered prisoners, gave them a sum of money, but Mum, indignant, immediately turned hers over to a missionary association.

From a conversation with Licinio Licini (born 1933); Monte Vidon Corrado, March 2001

Renato Corradini

George didn't want to go back to the war

I was a boy that September, only 14 years old, but I still remember what happened. I was living here with my family, in this house in Contrada San Paolo. There was a little copse below the vineyard, down at the bottom near the gully, and one morning as I was going to work in the fields I heard some strange noises from this piece of scrub. My curiosity aroused, I went to have a look and I found myself face-to-face with men in uniform. In faltering Italian they asked me if I could give them something to eat. One of them even asked for a cigarette, but I told him that I didn't smoke. However, I invited them to come to our house where we could find something to meet their needs.

One of them spoke Italian quite well but the others didn't, they were only able to say a few words. They were tall and thin, only one was short of stature, which meant that Mother was able to pass some of my clothes on to him. We gave them food and clothes to wear: clothes from my father, my uncle, and mine too. At that time everyone was poor and clothes were expensive, especially for us *contadini*, so we had very few clothes.

All three were English and they told us their names: Johnny was from London, George from Nottingham and Simon from Manchester. They had been hiding in the woods for three days after their escape from Monte Urano camp and they didn't know which direction to take. They were in bad shape. My mother, when she went to get their things after they'd changed clothes, noticed that they were full of lice, which infested the room. To get rid

153

of them we had to wash everything in boiling water – that was the only way to kill the bugs! A few days later we organised a collection among the neighbours and got hold of more clothes for all three of them.

One of them had a leg wound. It was disgusting, you could see the bone through the rotting flesh. It looked as if it was becoming gangrenous. My mother washed the wound right away and the stench of rotting flesh that emerged from the wound was unbelievable. Mum told us that if it were not treated immediately he was in danger of dying. We had a good relationship with our doctor, Dr. Francesconi, who lived at Magliano di Tenna. We were aware that he was an open fascist sympathiser but we still decided to risk it, because we couldn't let that man die slowly without having tried to treat him. My father went to call on him and the doctor arrived the next day. He asked a few questions and immediately took an interest in the wound, unable to conceal his concern. Then he began to clean up the wound: it was bloody, horrible and painful. George shook from head to foot. Drenched in sweat, he endured this enormous suffering because he knew it was for his own good. When he had finished, the doctor told Mum that she had to repeat this operation every day.

He warned us: "The wound must be kept clean. This will allow the skin to heal over, otherwise his condition will become critical."

Saying that, he bade us farewell.

Of course, it was possible that he could report us, in which case fascists and Germans would immediately swoop on our house. But this doctor was a gentleman who was only interested in the wellbeing of the prisoner. Besides, at that time everyone was a fascist: even my father had been forced to get a party membership card. On one occasion he had an argument with the Carabinieri: they wanted him to get a card for each member of the family, but he told them that it was expensive (you needed to buy the card, it was not free) and that, for a family of *contadini*, one card was sufficient.

There were 10 people living in our little house so there was no room for prisoners as well. So we spoke to our neighbour who lived just below us because we knew that he had a room. We asked if he would let them sleep there and then they could come to our house to eat. So that's how we arranged it: at night they were at the neighbour's and during the day they were with us.

They stayed here for several months and then "Giovanni" (Johnny), who spoke a little Italian, managed to make contact with other English escapers through a group in Cerquabella. Giovanni was a very capable person, he even went out during the day to go to Montegiorgio. Dressed in knickerbockers, like one of us, no-one could tell he was a foreigner. He also understood our dialect, but if someone engaged him in conversation he just answered with a few words so that he didn't let on where he came from.

That is how he was able to make contact with prisoners who were being sheltered by other families. Unfortunately there were also a couple of prisoners who were in hiding locally with a family of *contadini* and we heard they were getting drunk all the time and behaving badly. Our prisoners were really exemplary; they were always respectful and polite.

Around then we heard of a round-up by the Nazi-Fascists and the capture of some English prisoners and of young Italian draft dodgers, who all ended up in camps in

Germany. Seriously, the fear of being discovered was so strong. But after a few days everything calmed down again.

One evening, several of the prisoners – maybe 12 or 13 – were here in our house making arrangements for their departure. They were going to try and reach the Allied Front, by crossing the Maiella. They were eating the egg pasta that George had learned to make and which he often prepared: *moccolotti* [a Marche name for a type of pasta] – it was a pleasant diversion for him. He kneaded the dough and gripped the little machine with enormous satisfaction. That night Mum had killed a rabbit and she had cheerfully prepared a grand table. Nevertheless, there was a vein of sadness running through it all because they decided to leave the next day.

Well, they did leave, but John left a letter with us, saying that we should hand it over to the British as soon as they arrived.

It was almost Christmas.

George reappeared about 20 days later. We asked him what had happened and he said: "I don't want to go to war any more. The war is down there and I am sick of war." We didn't manage to get any news of the other two.

So he stayed with us until the Allies arrived in June, sleeping next door and being with us during the day. He gave us a hand in the fields; he was always helpful, even with the stable and the animals. He drew water from the well for the beasts to drink and he also tried to use a spade – although not very successfully, despite being a miner.

When the British arrived we went by bicycle to Fermo to their headquarters, where George asked for packets of cigarettes because he was an inveterate smoker. As requested, we delivered John's letter. But, instead of rejoining the British forces, George came back to our house and handed out cigarettes to everyone. He didn't want to leave; he must have been with us another couple of months.

During that period George was probably regarded as a deserter, and one time he arrived home in a rush, asking for help and a place to hide. We put him down in the hole underneath the barn, where we used to hide supplies. In the meantime, British and Polish soldiers arrived asking about a man who was on the run. Perhaps they had mistaken him for a fascist or something, but we were all dreadfully afraid.

Anyway, even though George didn't want to go back to the fighting, he still had to leave.

A little time passed, then, to our amazement and astonishment, the English command sent us about 30,000 lire and a parchment as a token of gratitude for the shelter given to prisoners during the war. Thirty thousand lire were really a lot for us farmers and that money allowed us to pay off some debt, but certainly what we did for the three Englishmen was only to help people in difficulty, with no other ulterior motive.

One of the nice things that I remember from those days was Johnny trying to woo my sister.

"Nella, I'll take you with me to England," he'd say.

"No, no," she would reply. "I've already decided that I want to be a nun!"

And that is what happened. As soon as she was 21 years old she left to enter the nunnery. This was against my father's wishes because he had tried to stop her following her vocation.

Filippo Ieranò

Of the three, the only one who wrote after the war was Johnny, who also visited us years ago with his wife and father-in-law. Even now, after such a long time, he continues to send me Christmas greetings and a calendar every year. Still, 50 years later, he sent us this year's 2001 calendar with his greetings.

From a conversation with Renato Corradini (born 1929); Montegiorgio, April 2001

Arduina Rossi

My poor mother fixed up a bed

I lived in San Cristoforo di Amandola. It took a good while to get from there to Servigliano on foot. If you think that it took three-quarters of an hour or more from Monte San Martino to Servigliano, it took at least two hours to walk from San Cristoforo. Two hours on the way there and two coming back: at least four hours in all.

Our family consisted of our parents and eight children. During the war three of my brothers were called up, one of whom was married with children.

The family had changed a bit because two of my sisters had left when they got married, but Florindo's wife and their three children had come to live with us because he had gone away to war.

After the news of the Armistice in 1943 everyone was happy and my dear Mum said: "Now my boys will come home." She was thinking of Florindo, who was a prisoner in Greece, and Alberigo, who was in Africa.

I remember that when Florindo arrived home after the war he said that he had eaten potato peelings to survive, no more than that. He had been starving.

Up here in San Cristoforo you didn't know what was going on in Servigliano. I had never been to the prison camp, although I had vaguely heard about the prisoners of war who were there.

Sometimes we walked to Servigliano to sell eggs. I remember that this took almost two hours, yes that's right, two hours. We weren't walking fast; you had to go slowly, with the egg basket on your arm.

159

I was just a girl and there was a lot I didn't understand. In the old days, girls weren't as smart as they are now. Nowadays 15-year-old girls are already big and sure of themselves.

I was the baby of the family and not very confident. We lived in the countryside and our poor Dad made us go to school only up to the third year, because our family was so large and you had to start working. A few days after the Armistice we heard that the prisoners had not returned to the camp, they had escaped, and this is when they went to the various families.

Two of them came to our house. We lived near the road; they were walking past and stopped to talk to us. They could speak a little Italian, just a bit, but they managed to make themselves understood very well.

They asked if we had any room for them.

At first my poor father and mother were afraid because so many people were wandering around the area in wartime, but then they decided to take them in for a few days. We gave them food and they were very happy and they thanked us. They ate with us, eating the same as us.

My dear old Mum fixed up two beds in a closet for them.

They came to work with us. They were willing to help with anything, although they didn't know the country ways. However, little by little they learned and we worked well together, like brothers. We were fond of each other: they respected us and we respected them.

It felt like one big family. Later on they left and I don't know if that was on their own initiative. I don't remember. Maybe they left to go to their own homes. I don't remember.

They stayed with us from September 1943 until the following spring. They were even with us when we killed the pig and our dear Mum cooked potatoes with pork rinds.

In winter there was little work. We could make bundles of firewood but it was not the season for hoeing and you couldn't go into the fields, but they were always willing.

After the prisoners had left, both the fascists and the partisans came to our house. The fascists arrived by truck and they killed people because they were terrified and were running away. They just shot at random at those poor people. One day they killed a young man, our neighbour, because they had seen him running away. But he was running because he was afraid they would arrest him and take him away as a prisoner, a long way away. Poor boy. He was a good-natured soul! As soon as he saw the trucks he started to run. Although he had managed to get far away, down to the scrub by the river, the fascists had binoculars and shot him anyway. The news spread immediately: "Iommi's son is dead!" "They have killed that poor boy!" A short while afterwards some fascists arrived at our house, in a truck, to carry out a search, but luckily the two prisoners had already left.

Partisans also came to our house, and they took away our animals. They were hiding above Piobbico in the mountains. One evening they surrounded the house – there were so many of them – and said that they wanted to take away the landlord's stuff.

In tears my poor mother said: "You're taking away everything we have, what will we do, this is all we have to live off!" But they replied: "We're not taking what is yours, only the stuff that belongs to the landlord." We were sharecroppers on the lands of the "Conte" (count), we "shared" with him. However, they took a "milker" and a cow, two beautiful beasts.

It was the responsibility of Florindo, my poor brother who had just returned from the war, to walk the two beasts up to Piobbico. The same thing happened to another farmer nearby: he had two more animals taken away. Florindo was out throughout that night, and when he came back in the morning he found us all crying, even his wife was crying. She was weeping because the partisans had taken away her husband as well as the beasts. However, we noticed that she had a roll of black cloth, a beautiful roll of cloth, something that you would see in a shop. The partisans had given it to her as a sort of compensation. It was delicate material. Although in wartime all fabrics were thin, this seemed like gossamer, very fine, something that would not last two minutes. Shopkeepers kept the good stuff under lock and key for fear of theft and only displayed the material that was less fine.

We also hid cheese and lard in among the wheat; it was a very big field so it would be very difficult to find the hole. We hid the linens in another hole in the cow barn, underground. We had dug that hole for the linen trunks because whatever they found they would remove, both the fascists and the partisans. My dear mother had already prepared a trousseau for one of my sisters who was going to be married, and for me too. I was 22 years old and I was going to be married the following year. We put all this stuff in the ground and then we covered it with tables and hay. It just looked like the animals' manger: no-one would manage to find it there. Sometimes the partisans even asked for money, but no-one had any money. But to get rid of them my poor Dad had to hand over his meagre savings.

Who knows if they really were partisans, or if they were actually thieves out to cheat poor people? No-one knew who they were. Some said they were partisans, but that some of them were exploiting the situation. The prisoners never came back to my house again. In those days there were no phones, you wrote letters to communicate. But, in any case, we heard nothing more. There were other families who took in prisoners. I know of a girl who lived below Amandola who became engaged to a Pole. There were several Polish prisoners in Amandola.

From a conversation with Arduina Rossi (born 1921); San Cristoforo di Amandola, July 1999

Lino Luciani

He liked to bring in the oxen

In September 1943 I was about eight years old. I was only small but some things have stuck in my mind.

Because I was only a boy I did not know that there was a prison camp in Servigliano, just as I didn't realise that there was such a thing as fascists and Germans. We were just afraid of all of them.

Servigliano is a long way from where I lived during the war and from where I live now, about 10 kilometers away.

I remember that a Slav came to our house. His name was Novak, a name that has stayed with me. Some time later an Englishman also turned up.

Novak was to stay for about a month and the Englishman, whose name I forget, only stayed a few days, perhaps a week. When they realised that they could be discovered, the English soldiers went on their way.

Novak showed up suddenly one day. He was about two metres tall, with a severe crew cut. He asked us if we could hide him for a short while. He was good, a really good man! It wasn't easy to take the decision to hide him, we would be putting ourselves at risk, but here we were faced with someone who was lost and hungry. There are those times when you just have to do something. All of us, everyone was in fear. It wasn't just for one or two of us, it was everyone.

There were six of us at home: Dad, Mum and us kids, and an uncle and his wife who didn't have any children yet because they were newlyweds.

Once we had decided to hide him my parents prepared a good hiding place in the stable. And he remained there at least a month, maybe more.

He worked with us. Yes, indeed. He liked to bring in the oxen and he did everything that was asked of him. In particular, he had the job of fetching water from the well, having rigged up the cart with the cows. He was skilful! Yes, he was good at agricultural work, he really was. He got the hang of things immediately and did everything asked of him.

At first we were all cautious because we were afraid that Novak might have been a spy for the Germans, that he might double-cross us; or perhaps he was a thief who could take away everything we owned, even though we had little enough in those days.

But Novak was also afraid because he knew that some families, through fear, had given up the prisoners they had taken in, preferring that to being arrested by the Germans and fascists.

We were also afraid that a spy would go and tell the fascists about the prisoner at our house. But the prisoners were also well-organised: almost always they managed to hear of when a raid would take place and they fled into the woods before the soldiers arrived.

It is true that we were really running a risk. If they found a prisoner in the house the Germans and fascists would immediately get everyone outside. And they did not mess around!

On second thoughts, Novak must have stayed throughout the winter, because that year there was masses of snow and he stayed in the barn, all warm. Yes, indeed, there was snow, lots of snow!

Filippo Ieranò

When the winter was over he left and we never heard from him again. Not while the war was still on, nor afterwards. We were very fortunate. While Novak was with us we never had any raids by the fascists and Germans, even though they were always prowling around.

One day, as the kids were coming home from school, a truck full of Germans passed by on the road. The soldiers shouted in German, interspersed with a few words of Italian.

Maybe they just wanted to stop them. Of course, what they said was incomprehensible to the children, one of whom was the girl who was to become my wife. They were all scared because they feared arrest and deportation. Somebody suggested that they should run away, but an older girl had the idea of raising their hands in the fascist salute. When they did that the Germans calmed down immediately and they let them go on their way.

It was often the fascists who accompanied the German convoys, although they tried not to be recognised as such. I remember one July, when we were working the land with the cows, we heard bullets whistling.

We were up high and the skirmish was going on down by the river. Then everyone started running in a mad panic; only my parents tried first to put the cows under cover.

I have wonderful memories of Novak. He also taught me a few words of his language and was so well-mannered. The Englishman, too, behaved correctly. But he found it more difficult to communicate with us so he used a lot of gestures to get his meaning across.

A People's Courage

In our area there were also other people who took in prisoners.

From a conversation with Lino Luciani (born 1935); Monte San Martino, August 2001

Luciano Iommi

"Run away, they are coming for you!"

In those September days I was 26 years old and I was a soldier in the paratroop unit in Viterbo, waiting to go to Sardinia. The major told me I had to go there because that had been selected as my destination. I was a lieutenant and, because I was an officer, I could get away with telling him that if it were a question of going by plane I would go immediately, but that they should not suggest that I go by boat. The Mediterranean was being patrolled by Allied ships and it was an absolute miracle if you managed to reach Sardinia by sea. I would definitely end up as fish food.

When we heard about the Armistice on 8 September I got cracking and gave permission to the soldiers on duty in the fortress of Viterbo to leave and return to their homes. I wanted to prevent the unit from falling into German hands. As it happened, a couple of days later, on 11 September, the barracks were occupied by German troops.

I decided to leave at the same time as the others. I took the train and by 12 I was at home. I encountered no problems on the way. On the contrary, I had the impression that at that time, when the Italian government was transforming from friend to foe, the Germans were solely focused on avoiding clashes and unrest. Among other things, many German soldiers came from Austria and they were not strongly motivated to continue a war from which they were beginning to emerge as losers.

I shed my uniform in the village. I was thinking of becoming a lawyer, as I had already graduated in law. So, after a few weeks, when the situation seemed calm, I decided to start working.

In this area there were prison camps at Servigliano, Monte Urano and Sforzacosta; the prisoners fled *en masse* from those camps. Some of them set out immediately to flee southwards, the others took refuge in the countryside locally. It was mainly the *contadini* who sheltered them.

In the law firm where I worked several young people came to ask if they should obey the call-up of the newly formed Republic of Salò. I advised them against it and suggested to all of them that they go into hiding.

But the local fascists kept checking on me, so much so that one day I had to do a runner and leave for the mountains.

Meanwhile a prisoner from the Monte Urano camp came to the house and asked for refuge. His name was Douglas. He was an Englishman. I don't remember clearly how he came to us, how the contact was made, but we decided to hide him in our home.

There weren't many of us in the house: my mother, my sister Jolanda and I, so there was room. Two of my brothers were away; one was missing in Yugoslavia and the other was a prisoner of the British in India. Another sister was already married. At the time my father was in hospital and my mother agreed without objection to having the prisoner in the house.

Before my escape the prisoner spent most of the time hiding in the house to avoid any trouble. Of course, he did go outside around the house a bit, but he hardly ever went further afield. Other neighbours also sheltered prisoners and sometimes they ran into each other.

Douglas spoke Italian quite well and we could communicate easily. He was a classic Englishman – tall and blond. He always made himself available for work on the farm. He watched and learned. There was no shortage of work because my father wasn't around, but he was never one to hold back.

I was forced to go on the run because it became known that I was an anti-fascist: I advised the young men not to obey the republican laws, so I was in the fascists' line of fire.

I was already at work at Scalazzi's law firm when one morning he rushed in all alarmed and told me: "Run away, they are coming for you. Just now the guard told me that they were coming to arrest you today."

The guard was a friend and, because he worked in the municipality, he knew all about the comings and goings of the fascists.

I fled through a side door and, at first, I hid not that far from home, near a neighbour. Then I went towards the mountains. I made the decision to go to the mountains because a group of partisans had set up there and the news had spread everywhere. I got in touch with some of the CLN (National Liberation Committee) leaders and among this large group I remember Marozzini, an old lawyer from Fermo. Sometimes to maintain links I had to go by bike from the mountains to Fermo, passing through San Angelo and San Elpidio.

After I had left, Douglas remained at our house for some time, always staying hidden. But as far as I know there weren't any particular searches by the Nazis.

A People's Courage

Many Slav prisoners had joined the partisans in the mountains. I knew some of them and one of them died at my side during a firefight. I was one of the commanders of the Armed Partisan Groups (GAP) in the area and, collaborating with the group from Penna San Giovanni, we had organised an ambush of the Germans. We had left very early in the morning, crossed the Tennacola and the Tenna, where the waters were low, and we arrived at the Parapina district of Servigliano. The plan was to attack a German troop carrier. Everything was ready. When we caught sight of the vehicle we sprang the trap. We only intended to grab weapons and the vehicle. Caught by surprise, the Germans didn't respond to the attack and, when we gestured for them to raise their hands, they obeyed immediately. Unfortunately, however, during the action some of the inexperienced members of our group were gripped by panic and stayed in the background, hidden among tall wheat, leaving just me and Franck, an ex-prisoner from Yugoslavia, to be discovered. There was a tragic outcome. Realising that there were only two of us, the Germans grabbed their weapons and ran away, firing at us. A bullet struck my comrade, who died immediately.

It was an ugly episode. As a GAP commander I could also have put the partisans on trial for cowardice because they had run away through fear instead of intervening. This left us exposed to German fire and caused the action to fail. But I did not want to proceed with a trial because now the Nazis were in retreat and there had already been far too much violence and death.

Towards the end of the winter a Polish escaper came to our house to ask for refuge. The situation was definitely not advantageous, but we opened our home to him too and he stayed until the Americans arrived.

Every now and then at night I would go home to see my parents again and I checked that everyone was pulling their weight. We also had animals and everyone had to play their part. During that long period a strong relationship arose between the Polish prisoner and my sister Jolanda; in fact, after the war, he returned to marry her and they left together for Argentina, in fact to Buenos Aires. My sister always wrote from there that she was happy and well. Sadly, a few years later she became a widow but she decided to stay in that faraway country.

When the Americans and the British arrived, Douglas was reunited with his people and he left, having thanked us for what we had done for him. We didn't hear anything of him for quite some time and then, a few months after the end of the war, he wrote to us that he was fine and, once again, he thanked us for everything.

After the Liberation I left everything that I had been involved with behind. I was not cut out for politics and I threw myself into the legal profession. Perhaps I was wrong, but at the time I thought I was making the right choice. I do have second thoughts, when I consider the political errors of that time and the shameful state of politics today.

But these are thoughts of an 85-year-old who is still surrounded by paperwork and folders, and who is trying to clean up and to throw away the old files. But that isn't easy, either!

From a conversation with Luciano Iommi (born 1917); Montappone, April 2001

Amelia Antodicola

He hid in the bell tower

Amelia Antodicola

I was about 22 when the news of the Armistice got out. Everyone welcomed it with enthusiasm, saying: "The war is over! The war is over!"

An old man, who understood things better than young people, said: "Let's hope that this is not the beginning of the end."

If I'm not mistaken it was a festival day, because in my village there is a little church where one celebrates Mary, mother of Jesus, on that very day. We went along and everybody was talking about the Armistice and how the Americans had already landed. Many of us were very happy but some were also expressing concern. However, everybody was hopeful that the war might finish. Instead,

173

the Germans began to show themselves, together with the fascists and also the partisans.

It was known that the partisans had organised themselves at Sarnano, which is why the fascists at Montelparo moved around freely. Their chief was a certain Roscioli, and what he hadn't done God alone knows.

When the camp at Servigliano was opened up, all the prisoners left: there were Americans, English, Slavs, Russians, a bit of everything. At first they went around the houses with a certain ease and many of them came to Montelparo. Only a few came to the village, though; most asked for refuge in the countryside instead. We lived in the centre of the village and the people there also mobilised to rescue the prisoners. So Dad and Mum said we could take one too. That was how we got to know Robert. Dad came into the house bringing this boy with him, who was always polite and well-mannered. We put him in a small room upstairs but he ate with us. He didn't speak much Italian. It was obvious immediately that he was an educated person. He was a handsome boy and tall, typically English. Our household consisted of Mum and Dad and five children. Elio, the oldest, had been captured by the Americans in Sicily.

On the day he arrived we gave Robert something to eat, then he got washed and put on civilian clothes. Just like a normal person. We treated him as one of the family. He was very happy.

In the early days, but only with care, he used to leave the house and meet his friends. But that all took place in hiding because the Germans and fascists began to be seen and there was a risk of reprisals. However, the partisans, who had set themselves up at Sarnano, met the prisoners every now and again. For several days prisoners arrived in the village, but they were taken into the countryside by the *contadini*, to keep them hidden. In the evenings they could generally move about more safely and they went back into the village to meet up and talk among themselves.

Robert always remained at our house and would go out only when one knew it wasn't dangerous. Some of the houses of the *contadini* were set on fire either because somebody had spied on them or because the Germans had found something compromising, something that made them think that a prisoner was hidden there.

There was also the case of an Englishman, David, an intellectual. I saw him shot outside the village. Poor man. That day, I and my sister were going home along a country lane. Suddenly we met David, who was running. As we knew him we gave him a friendly greeting: "Hi, David." But he merely responded with a wave of his hand and went on his way. A few minutes later, just as we had gone round a corner, we heard a rattle of gunfire. We hurried towards home, terrified. We saw in the village that everybody was alarmed. Back home we got to hear of the murder of David; clearly the news had preceded us.

David had been living with *contadini* in the countryside. We learned that on that day some German trucks had suddenly appeared on the track and that David had immediately fled so as not to be found. He had succeeded in going a good long way and it would have been difficult for the Germans to work out where he was hidden. There is still an iron cross at the spot where he was shot that commemorates him. He was buried in our cemetery but after the war his relatives took his corpse to England.

On the same day, the Germans also conducted a round-up in the village but, luckily, Robert hid himself in good time. Robert was married and had two children. He often talked to us about his family: he said that his wife, Pearl, was really good at looking after the house. During winter evenings we huddled round the fire, then we told our stories and he told us his. As the weeks passed he had begun to learn Italian. But, stupidly, I didn't listen to him when he said: "Amelia, I'll teach you English."

"What would I do with English?" I replied. He was always polite.

On one occasion, it was awful, about a hundred Germans surrounded the village because word had spread that Montelparo had become a partisan stronghold. It wasn't true because the closest one to us, if I'm not mistaken, was Sarnano. So, lots of them came. The sister of a big fascist who lived down the road tipped us off: she summoned my father, who was a locksmith, and on the pretext of getting him to mend the door she told him that the Germans were about to arrive.

Robert immediately fled towards the square and on entering the parish priest's house he hid in the bell tower. Everybody lent a hand to hide the prisoners, and the priest, Don Giovanni Mecozzi, also played his part. He pretended to know nothing, poor chap. On that occasion he bade Robert to be very careful: he was afraid that if the Germans discovered him they would set fire to the tower. The Germans were particularly nasty that day. They searched thoroughly, but without finding anything. Some of the soldiers even paused to admire the view of the valleys and mountains from the square beneath the bell tower, while Robert kept watch overhead.

What saved us was the intervention of a man named Vecchioli, who was from Rome and who had married a woman from Montelparo. This man, who spoke German, began to talk to the commander and finally succeeded in convincing him. He managed to persuade him that there were no partisans at Montelparo and that it was a quiet village that didn't present a danger. They therefore called a halt to the round-up but asked to be invited to lunch. A number of families were called upon to host three or four Germans in their homes and give them a good meal. Thus, while Robert stayed hidden at the top of the bell tower, four Germans came to eat at our house. In the afternoon, after drinking a little, they cheerfully began to sing in their own language and everything seemed normal. Finally, towards evening, they took to the road again.

I admit that in the house they were respectful, even if we were scared stiff. Certainly the Germans were better than the fascists, who were arrogant and vengeful. Sometimes we heard Republicans picking on and beating up young men who had not attended the military call-up, while Robert was at home shaking with anger.

On other occasions, if warned in time of the Germans' arrival, Robert and the few prisoners who were in the village would go and hide in the countryside, especially in a place called Lame, because it was full of grottos and gullies covered with scrub. Then, if the danger went on for some time, the *contadini* took them food and gave them news.

The greater danger, however, came from the fascists who, alarmed by the American advance, often used the Germans for personal vendettas.

In the summer of 1944 the German army began to withdraw. At times we saw convoys travelling along the main road and everybody feared the worst. But when they got below the village the soldiers began to sing in order to let us know they didn't have bad intentions.

When the Americans arrived, all the prisoners came outside and celebrated in the square. I think that they were summoned on the radio to join their various units and each of them made their own way. Robert, who had to present himself at Ascoli, went away but promised to return. When we said goodbye he was moved, but he kept his word. In fact he was the only prisoner at Montelparo to come back after the war. He began by sending us letters, then one day in the summer of '47 he came with his wife and children. Together we went to see the places where he used to hide; he pointed out to his wife the top of the tower where he had found shelter during a German raid, and the caves in the countryside.

We stayed in touch with him for many years, then the letters thinned out until they stopped. But recently, through a granddaughter of mine who knows how to use the internet, we managed to find out that he is dead and that his children live in Venezuela.

So much time has passed, what a lot of risks. We were always afraid we could be caught out. Robert, too, was worried on our behalf; he feared for our family. When we went to bed we used to think: "Who knows if they will come to check on us tonight." However, it never occurred to us to show him the door. Mum used to say: "Poor boys. This bloody, horrible war isn't their fault!"

In the days after the Liberation groups of partisans came to the village to seize the fascists who had collaborated with the Germans. One morning we heard someone call out loudly: it was Mario Snoriguzzi. In terror he told us that the partisans had been looking for him at home and that he was on the run. Mario was a fascist, but he wasn't like Roscioli; he was one of many, a fascist but not a fanatic. Shortly afterwards some partisans came looking for him, among then Angelici, from Servigliano, whom my father had trained to be a locksmith. They asked about Mario but Dad replied that there wasn't anybody and that they could leave with a clear mind. Thus we found ourselves hiding a fascist in the cellar, with the partisans on the ground floor.

So much time has passed.

Amelia Antodicola with her sisters in the 1940's

From a conversation with Amelia Antodicola (born 1921); Montelparo, July 2001

Editor's note: "David" was also known to the villagers as "Giorgio". These were the *noms de guerre* of Signalman Sidney Smith. Amelia's account differs in some respects from witness statements taken by the War Crimes Commission.

Abramo Marzialetti

A sanctuary inside a bundle of stacked wood

Abramo Marzialetti

I was born at Servigliano in 1930. In 1924 my family, which consisted of my parents, grandparents, paternal uncles, three brothers and a female cousin, moved to Montegiorgio. We lived in the countryside, a few hundred metres from the hills that dominate the Faleriense highway. We cultivated 15 hectares of land, as sharecroppers of course, and in truth we weren't short of what was needed to sustain us. However, every so often my father had to resort to certain subterfuges to prevent the fascist regime from taking what the family needed. Indeed, there was a compulsory contribution to the accumulation of agricultural products, for which we were registered. Despite all this, as I said, we weren't short of anything when it came to provisions.

This is where we found ourselves on 8 September. From the first days after the Armistice our army's disbanded soldiers began to pass by. They wandered around like poor stray dogs. They were scared, suspicious, hungry and in miserable tattered clothing. My father had a piece of bread for everyone and gladly added a word of comfort.

Some stayed for a few days and often lent a hand working in the fields. We let them sleep in the stable. Once refreshed to some extent they left again without a well-defined goal, almost always towards the north. During this time the partisans threw open the doors of the Agrarian Consortium at Piane di Montegiorgio and people nearby took advantage to appropriate to themselves God's bounty (grain) that was kept there. But the Nazi-Fascists went around the countryside looking for those responsible and for the stolen goods.

Not far from our house three innocent people who had sought to avoid capture were killed.

At the time we were looking after three of our soldiers. My father got them to hide in a wood a short distance away and they remained there for a couple of days. We children took them something to eat, until everything seemed normal and they were able to come back. They stayed on for another week or so. One day they decided to leave because, in the meantime, two prisoners from Servigliano had arrived.

"Our men" understood that to feed five persons had become particularly burdensome for our family, so they left. Another reason was that the newly arrived unfortunates had greater need of assistance in that, as foreigners, they were more exposed to danger. One was from New Zealand and the other from Australia. The first was a distinguished person, had a slim physique and seemed in poor health. My father didn't feel he could make him sleep in the stable and so he gave him my bed, where I usually slept with my brother. Together with the Australian we went down to the floor below (the stable).

The Australian impressed me in particular. He was lean and athletic. He was about one metre eighty tall and had lost half of three fingers on his right hand. He spoke our language quite well and explained that it had been caused by a burst of machine gun fire from a German officer. The latter had ordered him to raise his hands upon capture and let go the volley, mutilating the three fingers. Who knows how much truth there is in this, but the Australian added that the German general, Rommel, had been present at the scene. He said that he wasn't particularly fond of the British army because – especially at the Battle of Tobruk – the Australians were the most exposed while the eventual honours always went to the British.

A fortnight had elapsed since the arrival of these unlucky men when one evening, as it grew dark, two other poor chaps appeared. They were accompanied by my friend and contemporary, Emilio Vita, who lived, and still lives, in the hamlet of Piane di Montegiorgio; he was clearly scared by the risk he was running. This time they were Englishmen. One was called Giorgio [George], who said he was from London; he was about 204 cm tall and weighed 100 kg. The other was Jack, a Welshman of medium height with hair the colour of straw. Their appearance glaringly betrayed their Anglo-Saxon origin. While the former was mild, calm and chubby, the latter was very lively and, I would say, rebellious and stroppy. It was obvious that there was bad blood between them, but fate had obliged them to stay together.

"Big Giorgio", the Londoner, managed somehow to mitigate the Welshman's impetuosity and certainly contributed to him remaining safe. In fact Jack didn't want to stay with us but preferred to escape towards some unknown destiny. He was particularly annoyed by the fact that the New Zealander and the Australian were also there.

I would say that the only pleasant, relaxing and in fact hilarious moments were during lunch, which was almost always based on home-made spaghetti. They couldn't roll the blessed spaghetti around the fork; they never managed it, always ending by picking it up with their hands. That caused much hilarity.

Despite this enjoyable episode we understood perfectly that the Welshman and the Australian were incapable of getting on together. They teased each other constantly and one day, while they were lending a hand in the fields, they came to blows. The Welshman got hold of the Australian good and proper and gave him a beating; my father's intervention saved him from worse. "Big Giorgio" remained indifferent and did not deign even to watch the scene.

The episode certainly left an impression on the contenders and on the mind of my father. Indeed, it added to the risk posed by the Germans; the violence between the two could have more dramatic consequences.

After a few days of obvious tension the Australian mentioned to my father that, together with the New Zealander, he would leave our house. They went the same day and my father breathed a sigh of relief. We heard no more of them, not even in the years that followed.

Filippo Ieranò

The two Britons now felt safer and looked after. Meanwhile the partisans were in great form. They had got to the point of ring-fencing the Faleriense highway with tree trunks in order, they said, to slow down the German army's retreat. At that time, too, the German Red Cross was attacked and a soldier found on board [the vehicle] was killed. The Nazi-Fascists were highly vigilant in these situations. One could say that we felt them breathing down our necks. My father was very anxious.

The two unfortunate former prisoners spent all day hiding in the wood and we children risked great danger to take them pieces of bread. They used to come back to catch a few hours' sleep in the stable, but not always. They would leave again at dawn. The situation had become unsustainable. Nobody knew what was the best thing to do.

Necessity, however, sharpens the wit. In the large courtyard of our house there was a bundle of stacked wood. My father built a sort of cage out of strong wooden planks, big enough to "accommodate" two people. He covered it with a waxed sheet, leaving a hole so that they could enter on all fours. He made a bed consisting of straw and thin blankets and, from that day on, this became the residence of the two Britons. I must make clear that one could only lie down in this cage. Of course, with the utmost caution, the poor men had to go outside, especially for their personal needs. Preferably they did this at night.

The danger persisted and became more and more pressing. The Germans and the fascists, angry at the events that were occurring, became really determined. They raided our house several times and once it was really nasty. That time, unusually, we were taken by surprise and found them already there. From where we lived it was possible to spot arrivals because our house was in the hills and looked over all the approaching roads. It wasn't the case on that occasion. I can still see the scene. The two Britons were no more than 50 metres away from the house and my grandmother, Nicolina, was in front of the chicken coop situated on the road along which the Germans were advancing. With admirable quickness of wits and reflexes, the old lady pretended to stumble and fell on the ground right in front of the soldiers' sidecar. She yelled, as if with pain. This alerted the two prisoners who slipped into their hiding place a few paces away.

The two Nazis behaved well. They asked for some fresh eggs and, after receiving them, to our great relief they left without conducting a search. I had already got the impression that they didn't want to see anything.

There were good people even among that lot.

By now it was nearly February and those two wretches had been in that stack for more than three months. One could feel the tension and, unfortunately, it would still have to go on for a long time. If I remember rightly, the army of liberation arrived towards the end of June 1944. By then those people had been caged for about eight months.

The big day came and the nightmare ended. The two men had survived and were naturally delighted. Their looks conveyed the sense of immense debt that they owed our family. We had certainly saved the lives of two men and the possibility arose that other mothers far away might be able to embrace their sons again.

Notwithstanding the palpable atmosphere of joy, happiness and freedom that we all sensed, there was something that made us anxious.

Along with these unfortunate men we had undergone a severe trial for about eight months. Fondness and affection had developed unconsciously and they were reciprocated. The tribulations had embedded these sentiments. The moment of repatriation, so long awaited, had arrived for these men. And, perhaps selfishly, this made us sad. It was a "happy sadness".

Collection centres were set up as July approached, and a few days later we accompanied them to one of these places at Piane di Montegiorgio.

All of us went to say farewell to these men. Only my grandmother and my youngest brothers stayed at home. Some of our neighbours who knew of the risks run by my family also went. Like all farewells it was sad, but this one was particularly so because it reminded us of all the suffering and of a period of our life that was ending.

This feeling of dejection and depression lasted for some time and then slowly life resumed its course.

They wrote to us periodically for some time, then no more. And so closed a period of our lives which, for want of a better word, had been really worthwhile.

If I remember rightly we didn't receive anything from the British state. Our charity remained anonymous and therefore was more valuable. I and my three brothers who live at Porto Sant'Elpidio are the surviving protagonists of this story.

I don't have photos or addresses of our British friends because time has destroyed everything!

A letter from Abramo Marzialetti, Montegiorgio, March 2002

Cesare Viozzi

They set it on fire

There were 28 of us in the house in this period. We lived halfway between Santa Vittoria in Matenano and Ponte Maglio; four families together, all in the same house. The prisoners were spread out in the countryside; they came to ask for help, a bit here, a bit there. So my parents decided to take in two Americans called Martin and Robert, and the family expanded to 30 people.

I don't remember exactly what towns they came from. I only know that Robert spoke of having only two more years to go before becoming a doctor. He was tall and strong while the other was a bit smaller. During the time they were at our house they taught all of us some American words, and I still remember the numbers: one, two . . . up to 12. The rest I've forgotten. They did this to pass the time, because Robert spoke Italian well. I don't know where he'd learned it, but, being a doctor, he learned quickly.

They were given a crib in the stable, which was hidden by hay and the animals. They came inside with us for meals. They only hid in the stable in the evening, but during the day we were always together. Robert, in particular, always showed himself ready to lend a hand; he was with us when the animals were tended to or when there was something else to do. The other wasn't around as much on those occasions. They stayed with us for a long time.

We spent Christmas together. There wasn't enough room for everyone in the house because we were so many, so we went to play cards in the stable. When it got late we returned to the house and they hid behind the hay. Everyone liked them, so much so that, on certain occasions, because Robert smoked and it wasn't easy to find cigarettes, an uncle who is now dead went into town and somehow managed to find him some. Robert always promised that as soon as the war was over he would come back with the family, and he invited us to go to see him in America. He was a really nice person.

Early one morning we saw German troops coming along the road towards Santa Vittoria. We were scared and immediately made the two prisoners escape and they hid themselves in a gully. Word went around us *contadini* that the Germans were withdrawing. As soon as all seemed quiet we told them that they could return.

After a bit, while we were at the table having breakfast, we realised that two soldiers on two motorbikes, with sidecars, were coming in the direction of our house. No-one expected anything like this, and in fact the two Americans were with us at the table. We didn't even have time to think of any solutions before the two Germans began to shout, ordering us to come out and threatening us with their weapons. We never understood how, but they recognised the two Americans immediately and they seized them.

It could only have been that a spy informed them. Otherwise it was impossible that they could have recognised the prisoners, dressed like us, in such a short time. Threatening them with their weapons, they made Robert and Martin get into the sidecars and they left. We kept watching; we were very frightened. They seemed to stop in a little wood on the river Aso, near Ponte Maglio. A few seconds later the Germans fired several shots. A little later we learned that the Americans had been murdered. Then the two soldiers got on their motorbikes and returned to our house. I ran off with some of my cousins, all boys, and hid behind a hedge. The Germans made everyone come out of the house, and my parents were even forced to carry out into the farmyard a poor old aunt who had been bedridden for years.

One uncle wanted to do something but, as the weapons were pointed at them, his brothers told him to keep still; there could have been a massacre with all the women and children in the farmyard. We boys, who had managed to flee, watched everything from afar. The Germans immediately began to set fire to everything, entering the rooms and torching things. My poor, desperate mother, notwithstanding the threats, beat at the flames trying to put them out.

Arriving at the room of the *vergaro*, they shut themselves in and remained inside so that the room didn't fill up with smoke. Every family had a *vergaro*; among us it was an uncle who kept the accounts for the whole household of four families. If there were shoes to buy, clothes or other things, it was always him who dealt with it. There were 28 of us and someone had to be in charge. In that room money was hidden, and we recovered about half of it, pulled from the flames. Whoever told on us had given the Germans very precise information.

They loaded all our goods on to their motorbikes. Given that we had butchered four pigs some months before, there was a lot of stuff. They also set fire to the stable, but luckily my uncles managed to save the animals that were inside. Then, as the women screamed, they pointed at the haybarn. Waving their weapons around and shouting, they indicated to an uncle that he was to get something. He was terrified because he had hidden his double-barrelled shotgun under the haystack and he thought the Germans knew. He was almost resigned to giving it to them when he realised that they only wanted to make him pick up an armful of hay to help everything burn better. If my uncle had picked up the gun, who knows what would have happened.

Before leaving they fired bursts of machine gun fire at the walls of the house and maybe even threw hand grenades at the windows, terrorising everyone and shattering the glass. Another soldier came and, seeing that we had a horse, ordered us to hand it over. The retreating Germans took everything! The fear was such that not even our three dogs barked.

The very same day a line of vehicles on the road came to a halt, presumably because one of their lorries had broken down. We saw some soldiers get down and leave the lorry behind. As soon as they had disappeared from view some boys who lived a few hundred metres from my house went to look around near the lorry. After about half an hour, while we were still dealing with the fire, we heard the sound of motorbikes coming from Santa Vittoria; several soldiers were coming back for the lorry. On seeing the boys they opened fire, killing two of them. It was a tragedy: they were 16 and 17 years old, the sons of *contadini*.

The next day a farmer brought the bodies of the two Americans to Santa Vittoria by horse and cart, for burial. The ridiculous thing was that he claimed payment from us for the transportation. Crazy stuff. The house was badly damaged, the flames made the roof unstable and the frame was almost non-existent. All summer we had to carry out difficult renovations.

There were plenty of prisoners hidden around and about, but it was our house on which the Germans took revenge. Luckily our neighbours helped us out. By hook or by crook we managed to carry on, but it was hard!

Several years later, Martin's and Robert's relatives came to take their bodies from the cemetery at Santa Vittoria back to their own country. Our family suffered the most in the vicinity, but no-one ever regretted having given hospitality to those poor boys.

From a conversation with Cesare Viozzi (born 1932); Santa Vittoria, July 2001

Filippo Ieranò

The perspective changes in the final part of this collection of stories. The narrators are two former escaped prisoners and a Jewish lady who had been a young girl in the 1940s; all three received a welcome in the Tenna Valley. While the accounts of James Keith Killby and Carla Bassani (*née* Viterbo) are the result of my interviews with them between 2000 and 2001, Manuel Serrano's text consists of extracts from a short autobiographical memoir written in the 1960s when the author was living with his wife at Servigliano.

Keith Killby

I thought it was a miracle

Keith Killby

My first sight of Italy was when I laid eyes on the coast of Sardinia through a submarine periscope. Unfortunately, six days after we reached the shore in a dinghy, we were captured and held in a concentration camp in Sardinia. From there we were taken to La Maddalena, then on to Naples, Rome, Porto San Giorgio and finally to the PoW camp at Servigliano.

Two weeks later we heard about the Armistice and immediately we tried to contact Italians so that they could help us escape: there were 3,000 of us. Confusion abounded so we decided to make a hole in the wall of the camp – which you can still see now, even though it has been repaired – and we started to climb through it. Some Italian soldiers fired their rifles into the air; then, in the chaos, the order was given to everyone to escape, both prisoners and guards.

At last I was free! We broke up into a small group, as everybody was doing. I was with some of my friends who had been captured with me. We wanted to make our way slowly southward and in the meantime we asked for help from Italian families living nearby. We were very surprised at how they helped us. It was incredible! I remember on one occasion while I was with two Americans on the hills near Monte San Martino that we saw a woman come out of a small house and signal to us to wait for her. A few minutes later I thought it was a miracle when I realised she was coming to bring us food.

It is incredible how everyone helped us!

The Germans were searching for us so I and my companions decided to stay in hiding for a few weeks. Then we set off towards the south and the mountains, passing through many places on the way. Unfortunately the two Americans and I were recaptured by the Germans at Agnone, close to the Molise area. We were held in a house for the night, with three of them. In the evening we ate together and drank some wine; the idea came to me to encourage the Germans to drink more than me and around midnight I heard them snoring. So I got up very slowly, holding my shoes, and went over to the window. As soon as I opened it I could see that it was too high up. So I decided to get down by jumping from balcony to balcony and in that way I managed to escape. I continued my journey on foot for a week and then met an elderly woman who would come early in the morning to my hiding place in a wood, bringing me food to eat. You had to take care to stay out of sight of all the Germans, who were everywhere.

However, I had to set off on my travels again so I asked for civilian clothes, which were not easy to find due to my height. And shoes were a particular problem. One night I went to the house of a very poor family. The grandmother immediately invited me to eat boiled potatoes and pears with them – that was all they had! I slept in the hay with the children but the next morning I moved on as it was very dangerous.

Upon reaching a short but very steep hill I realised that I had a temperature due to malaria. I was too weak to carry on and was spotted by a group of Germans who captured me. I was very weak and was taken by truck to Regina Coeli, my first "hotel", in Rome. There I bumped into a small priest, also a prisoner, whom I recognised because he used to visit us at Servigliano with firewood hidden under his robes so that we could make a fire and warm up. I spoke to him but he told me I had to pretend to not know him because the Germans had taken him prisoner as well.

From Regina Coeli they transported me to Germany, where I was liberated by the Russians.

I returned to Italy 18 years later and, while I was walking in the countryside around Monte San Martino, I met an elderly woman and we started talking a bit. She then explained to me that she too had helped an escaped prisoner. I added that there were many prisoners to whom the Italians had given help, but she specified that it was a nurse. I was a nurse! Then I recognised her, 18 years later. She then remembered a silly comment I had made at the time: I had asked her what she was holding in her hands and when she told me it was a bandage (*fascia* in Italian) I had said that I didn't want to learn that word as it sounded too much like "fascism". All this came back to us 18 years later.

Since then almost always I have come back twice a year. I have friends everywhere – Naples, Milan, Rome – but I prefer to return to my valley, between Monte San Martino and Penna San Giovanni, where I hid for the first time.

I will never be able to forget how much the Italians helped us! Above all, it was the poorest households that always tried to give us something. The families who did this were taking huge risks and sometimes they were shot for having helped us.

Last year I met a New Zealander who had also been a PoW on the run and he told me he had returned to Italy some time ago to pay his respects to two brothers who had been shot for helping him and some other PoWs on the run. It made me realise how we could all have been the cause of reprisals because when the Germans discovered someone had helped us they would shoot them on the spot.

Some time ago an English friend told me how he had gone back to the place where he had been sheltered while on the run. He asked around in order to find the house where he had hidden and he was directed to speak to a certain lady. The next day he met her and she said to him: "Even though I was a little girl, I remember three PoWs with a dog who came to our house. The day after they left the Germans arrived and shot my parents."

He was one of those three PoWs.

A People's Courage

It was an incredible thing to hear but there are so many stories like this – stories of generosity and suffering.

From a conversation with James Keith Killby, former British prisoner of war; Comunanza, April 2000

Manuel Serrano

The partisan from Brooklyn

Manuel Serrano

Two months had passed since the tragedy of Pearl Harbour when I volunteered for the paratroopers and was sent on a training course at Fort Benning, Georgia. After a few months we were sent to England for a while and then we participated in the invasion of North Africa.

Our first mission was to blow up a bridge, but on 27 December 1942 we were captured and taken to Tunis, where they took us on an Italian ship called the Zeno, destined for Palermo.

After two hours we arrived by train at Servigliano. Coming from Porto San Giorgio, people seemed more cordial there – they even offered us bread, despite the opposition of the Carabinieri present.

We set off, knowing the place we were headed for could be no worse than Camp 98 in Sicily. It was hot. There were many civilians watching us, especially girls, one of whom had panther eyes[1] and stared at us menacingly, but I didn't pay her any attention. On the other hand, these people did not shout at us or spit on us, as had happened earlier, particularly in Naples.

When we arrived at the camp our first impression was positive: everything seemed clean enough. Even the few English prisoners we met seemed clean and tidy. We were certainly relieved, because we were afraid of finding filth, as in the other camps.

A Carabiniere called our names and gathered us together to take us to another gate, where we saw many prisoners, all of them British. They greeted us with shouts and gestures and threw us some packets of cigarettes.

It is difficult to express our joy: it was the first time we had seen so many cigarettes since we had been caught.

Our dreams finally came true in September 1943 when we heard of the signed Armistice. We all escaped from the camp, heading towards the Tenna river, which had little water and many stones. After walking hidden through the countryside we arrived at a farm, about two miles from Penna San Giovanni. Some *contadini*, seeing us, told us to come in and they hid us in the stable. There were five of us: two Americans, Bob Sullivan of Albany N.Y. and me, and three Poles whose names I don't remember.

We stayed in that house about three months, not knowing where to go or what to do. We paced around the farm but didn't dare to go far away: it was too risky to go further.

Luigi, the farmer who hosted us, worked the land with his daughters, while his wife took care of the stable. They didn't have modern farm equipment and used a traditional plough pulled by oxen, as their ancestors had for centuries.

The view was beautiful, and all around you could admire medieval villages resting atop the hills. The population centres were occupied by fascists and Germans, so the peasants had moved to their homes in the countryside. Servigliano, with its grim prison camp, was the only village located below, in the valley.

I was tired of doing nothing and became more impatient by the day. [. . .] One day I decided to leave but, while we were drinking a cup of tea in the kitchen, Adriano signaled me to shut up: some fascists, maybe five or six, were standing in front of the house asking for information about a prisoner.

As soon as I realised the situation I left stealthily by the back door that opened on to a field of wheat, where I remained hidden until, to my great relief, I saw them leave. Then, after a quick goodbye, I walked away towards the mountains. It was with regret that I left this family that had shown me affection and risked much, because the fascists threatened that anyone who hid or helped escaping prisoners would be "put to the wall".

The road to the mountains was long, and when night fell I stopped at a farm where I asked to sleep in the barn. Instead, the peasants invited me to the kitchen and gave me a bowl of soup. I was beginning to get used to the friendliness of the people. In that house Matilde lived with her child and elderly father. She was quite a young woman, with large brown eyes and white complexion; she came from a neighbouring area, Falerone, but by marriage she went to live with her husband on the farm. It had not been easy for her to get used to the laborious work in the fields and, in addition, she had to endure a mother-in-law who constantly imposed her will.

She asked me where I came from. Sensing that I was an American and that I escaped from the Servigliano prison camp, she told me that they had also kept two English airmen for three months.

She told me her husband had been taken prisoner by the Germans and that she could not get any news. As she was telling me, we heard the dogs barking: a man walked briskly toward the house. As soon as he saw Matilde looking out the door he told her there was a German patrol on the street. Immediately she came back to warn us. Then the father looked at me, as if asking for help, but what could I do? I was on my own and a wanted man. To avoid problems I left immediately – without being able to say goodbye and thank them as they deserved – and walked away quickly into the brush, not stopping until I got to the partisan command.

Some time later we learned that the Germans had killed an Allied prisoner on the run and that they had also managed to find the house where he had been hiding, taking away a girl with her child and the father, who was about 80. People said they would shoot them and it worried me. I did not know for sure if it was Matilde and her family.

The fascists and the Germans, retreating under the pressure of the Allies, sought the fleeing prisoners more fiercely, knowing they must be not far from the Tenna Valley.

[. . .] There were very hard days during which the partisan gang which I commanded was continually attacked by fascists and Germans. We decided to split up in order to find shelter and cause them to lose our tracks. The cold was intense and one night it snowed like it had not snowed for 20 years. The first consequence for me was a rapid worsening of the cold I had, that had also perhaps produced a more serious infection.

During the day I couldn't get close to any house and at night I went to sleep in an old stable, but, despite the difficulties, I was convinced I would succeed in my assignment.

More days passed and my health situation remained the same: I needed medicine and maybe I had pneumonia. I prayed to God for time to do my duty and avenge the three friends betrayed and killed because of those girls. At the same time I asked His forgiveness for what I should have done, remembering the teachings I had learned as a young Catholic. Precisely for this reason, perhaps, it was His intention to keep me ill.

But, thinking back to Angela's eyes, when she looked at us prisoners with hatred, I noticed a certain softness, which also remained in our memories. She was beautiful, but everyone agreed the most beautiful thing about her were the two incredible black diamonds that shone in her face. But it was very disturbing that she could hate so much.

I remember that, when I was a prisoner, I asked to work outside just to get to know this beauty I had heard about. I managed to get a good look at that girl: it was true, nothing was comparable to those wonderful eyes! I paused, enchanted by her, until a guard ordered me to walk on.

Day by day I noticed the hatred in her eyes slowly fading, her gaze becoming more human, and one day I even detected the faint outline of a smile.

The other prisoners, seeing the way I looked at her, made fun of me and that was the last day they let me work outside the camp. Those who continued to work outside told me the girl was always in the same place and her eyes continued to be full of hate.

[. . .] I was a guest of the Cutini family when, one morning, the Germans came. All would have been lost but for the sudden intervention of a woman who, working with a pitchfork, covered me with straw. Then, as soldiers entered, she continued pitching straw to the animal crib, knowing full well where I was. She jabbed into the straw a couple of times to show that there could not be anyone beneath. The Germans often fired into the straw, but perhaps, seeing the woman at work as normal, they assumed no-one was there and left. I will never forget that that woman's quick-wittedness saved my life.

There was so much snow that we all stayed put and, thanks to being given warm wine, I was rid of the pneumonia in two months.

I knew nothing about the girl, or about the marshal of the Servigliano prison camp. I was looking for him, too, because he killed a six-month pregnant woman and her husband who were trying to take some linens from the camp the day we fled.

I had committed myself to finding the girl and the marshal, but the more time passed the more I seemed to lose track of them.

Fortunately, at that time the Poles and English arrived. For me it meant our battle had been won. I presented myself at my command and the captain told me our work in Le Marche was over; but whoever wanted to could go north to fight behind enemy lines.

I returned to Servigliano. For the first time I could look everyone in the face; however, I knew the biggest criminals had gone north with the Germans.

I went to the public balcony and spoke to everyone, asking those who had sided with the Germans to come to the public square within half an hour, otherwise I was going to seek them out and kill them.

Pretty quickly about 40 men had gathered near the municipal building, praying and crying. They asked for forgiveness and said they had been forced to do what they had done.

I had them put in jail.

Even the Servigliano police captain came forward and told me: "I am at your service in any way that I may be useful to you."

"So, give me your revolver because you will not need it in prison. What you are saying to me you no doubt also told the Germans," I replied, and added: "Take him away!"

In the middle of the night, I was told, 10 partisans had surrounded a house inside the village. It seems that Angela had returned and was hiding there. It was the moment I had been waiting for.

When I arrived at the house I ordered them to open the door. An elderly woman greeted me in tears.

By simply looking into the old woman's eyes I knew that she was Angela's mother.

My heart was cold: it was finally time for justice. She did not deserve to live and I intended to shoot her.

I entered and, the other side of the table, I saw two people I knew well. Angela looked at me fixedly with the same cruel eyes, full of hate. The other one was wounded.

Tension in that room was very high, like in a court of justice. The trial was being held in silence.

Only the old woman was crying. It was she who broke the silence by saying: "My Angela did not know the consequences her actions had on the prisoners. She did what she did only once and never again. Please do not hurt her."

"My companions, before dying, had also asked for clemency – in vain," I said. "There was no mercy for them! Their families will wait for them – in vain. Yet they fought for everyone's freedom!"

Hearing these words, Angela burst into tears.

"She must die," I continued.

I had just finished speaking these words when the door opened. It was Mrs Cutini, who had often hidden me. Crying, she said to me: "No, Manuel! No, Manuel! I am her godmother. It's true, she has been foolish, but for God's sake. No, Manuel!"

Then I understood why the hunt had been so difficult.

Angela cried in Mrs Cutini's arms.

Still with the gun in my hand, I addressed the wounded boy. Because I knew he had been with the partisans, I asked him: "And what are you doing here?"

He replied: "I am her brother and I have nothing to say – neither for nor against it! I know the law. Proceed then as you will."

It was unbelievable – that partisan, who had so bravely distinguished himself, was her brother.

As I looked around, my companions were calmer as they looked at Angela and her brother. It was certainly a difficult decision to make, and I pondered what to do.

I looked out the window and saw who really had the power to judge: the sun. It was already in the sky, a big fireball, and it announced that the new day would be beautiful.

I lowered my hands and put the revolver in my pocket. Without saying a word my companions and I slowly began to leave. I felt they, too, were satisfied with the decision I had made. I was about to leave the room when I felt someone grab my hand as she tried to kiss it.

A crowd had gathered outside, everyone fearing the worst. As soon as we came out, many rushed into the house.

That was the last time I saw Angela and her beautiful eyes.

By now my desire to go home was growing stronger, to resume my life: to walk freely, to shower every day, to eat three times a day.

While I was thinking of these things, I heard someone calling me: "Serrano, Serrano."

"What's happening?"

Some comrades replied: "The marshal of the camp has arrived!"

When I heard those words I went crazy: I grabbed my paratrooper jacket, which always brought me good luck, and in minutes I was in the town square.

It was really him: tall, greying hair, and in civilian clothes. He, along with the fascists and the Germans, had been responsible for the murder of that poor pregnant woman.

The people gathered round knew that this time there would be mercy for no-one. The marshal had not yet seen me. I drew close to him and said aloud: "Marshal, do you remember me? I'm Serrano!"

I was behind him and he whirled around. As soon as he saw me he started to stammer something, but I did not let him say anything: I punched him so hard that he fell to the ground. He got up immediately and a fierce struggle began. The crowd shouted "Give it to him! Give it to him!" because he was really hated, but no-one had had the courage to do anything before I arrived. The fight continued and there was blood everywhere.

Now it was he who could take it no more, and he called out: "Help! Help!"

I hit him again, reminding him of the children he had turned to orphans, of [their] mother and father. Fresh in my mind was the story that made me want to kill him: the poor woman on the ground dying. Her husband lifting her while the Germans, who did not understand what was happening, ordered him to leave – the man embraced her until a barrage of machine gun fire killed them both.

This dog was now asking for forgiveness and help.

While he was on the ground I saw him put his hand in his pocket. In a flash I was on him and managed to wrest from his hand the revolver he was pulling out. As soon as the crowd saw the weapon there was a general stampede in flight. I was on my knees with his gun in my hand, about to deliver justice by shooting him, when I heard the voice of a child cry out: "Daddy, Daddy, what are you doing?"

The little girl approached and took my hand, screaming in fear: "What are you doing to my father?"

I stopped to look at those tiny fingers, her hands, her thin arm, and her innocent face looking at me. Her eyes were swollen with tears. There was also another, an older girl, who sobbed in fright.

In the square no-one breathed. Everyone looked at us: the two girls, the wretched man, and me.

Looking at the girls, I stood up slowly. The man on the ground was covered in blood, but I too was wounded and my jacket stained red.

I backed away and the silence was broken by a friend, who said, "Manuel, are you hurt? Come!"

The crowd quietly began to murmur. They took me to a bar, thinking I was seriously injured, but I only had pain in my hands and fingers. While I was surrounded by friends they told me that the marshal had been taken away.

From the unpublished manuscript of Manuel Serrano

1. References in this extract to the girl with the "panther eyes", identified by Serrano later in the story as Angela, are clarified in his full, possibly embroidered, account. It appears that Angela hated the Allies because they had killed her father, a postman, while strafing a road. Serrano suspected that she had informed on his hosts, the Cutini family, and he also wanted to avenge the deaths of three friends who had been betrayed.

Carla Viterbo

Dirty Jew, don't pick my flowers!

Carla Viterbo

On 8 September 1943 I was in Venice. The fascist race laws had already been in force for years, so we were really uneasy. Some friends of my father came to tell us to run away because terrible things were taking place in Germany and the same would probably happen in Italy as well. So we thought of going south, to Ancona, where we knew some people, and then further on down to the Allied lines.

We managed to take a train, because we still had some freedom of movement, although the racial laws that had been imposed in '38 had pushed us into a life on the margins of society. My father had been forced to leave his job as a public works surveyor and my brother and I were expelled from school.

We got to Ancona without any particular difficulty and there we made a brief stop. My father talked to some of his friends. They recommended that he should carry on further south, to Porto San Giorgio, where it would be possible to stop for a while. That would also be safer.

We got on to the train again and arrived in Porto San Giorgio, where we rented a house from some fishermen. This situation was no good for anyone, especially for us because we didn't have much money and, as well as paying the rent for the house, we had to buy food. We had ration cards which did enable us to get food, but the cards had names on them which was risky for us. But we had no option, especially since some people had assured my father that we would be safe. I don't remember their names, but they told us that we could relax there.

Nevertheless, one October morning four Carabinieri turned up and surrounded the house, announcing that we were under arrest. They took us to their headquarters at Porto San Giorgio. Here they allotted a number to each of us. If I remember correctly, my father got the number 16, my mother 17, my brother 18 and I got 19. We stayed there for a few hours with the other Jews who had been arrested; they were mostly former internees. Then they handed us over to the Germans who took us by truck to Servigliano. There can't have been many of us because we all managed to get in the back of the vehicle.

Once we had arrived in Servigliano they made us get out of the truck in the square in front of the camp and they handed us over to the Carabinieri. They moved us inside the camp walls. The camp was almost deserted;

there were no Allied prisoners because they had all managed to escape a few days before.

My family was assigned a room in the infirmary. This was a frightful experience since the place was infested with bugs that tormented us from head to foot. I don't know if the conditions in the camp were the same when the Allied prisoners were there. Perhaps everything had fallen into such disrepair because the buildings had been deserted between the time of the soldiers' escape in mid-September and our arrival in early October. Nevertheless, the fact remains that conditions were terribly unhygienic. In fact the infirmary was not a hut, it was one of the few brick buildings in the camp. The other Jews were put in other rooms in the infirmary or in small huts nearby, rather than in the bigger spaces with bunk beds. Some were also housed in the former Command building, near the entrance to the camp.

When we were inside the camp walls we were prisoners, but some of us were allowed to go outside, accompanied by some Carabinieri.

We had nothing to do. My mother taught me to use a needle and thread and we darned socks – we even did that for the Carabinieri. I learnt it a little just to pass the time.

I worked with a young Russian boy who was about the same age as me, carrying out various tasks under adult supervision. Later he was murdered in a concentration camp in Germany.

Some of the detainees had responsibilities in the kitchen and they took turns to prepare meals under the watchful eye of the Carabinieri. However, the food was really dreadful: for the most part it was beans and peas that were full of maggots. The sickening stench of that slop is really indescribable. Sometimes, because food was so scarce, they allowed some of us to go round from house to house to beg for a piece of bread. The guards always came with us because they were afraid that we would run away. It was distressing to have to beg for food, but sometimes we did manage to get hold of something.

The guards teased my father, calling him "Signor Capitano" because he had been a captain in the Italian army in the First World War. He was appointed "Chief Toilet Cleaner".

We weren't allowed to work outside the camp so contact with local people was practically non-existent. During the winter the cold was dreadful and we had some really tough days: there was no water and we had to melt snow to get something to drink. Luckily we found the Allied prisoners' blankets in the huts and my mother made me a coat, because I was growing and nothing fitted me any longer. After all, we had very little with us when we escaped from Venice and none of us had imagined that we would have to face such a hard winter in those conditions. I had clogs that were patched with pieces of blanket.

During that time, contact had been established with the partisans and former Allied prisoners who wanted to have the camp bombed in order to allow us to escape. But my father and the other adults advised against it for the moment because it would have been hard to escape in such deep snow.

At the end of the winter, people from Tripoli in Africa were also interned in the camp, as well as some parents of young draft dodgers, who had chosen to go into hiding rather than enlist in the Republican army to fight alongside the Nazis.

A People's Courage

Once when I was coming back to the camp, as always accompanied by the Carabinieri, I picked a flower near the entrance outside the gate. Quick as a flash a child, who must have been the son of a Carabiniere, appeared and said to me: "Dirty Jew, don't pick my flowers!"

This sentence stuck with me, because it made me understand that the hatred of us Jews was taught in homes and within families.

However, among all those people who hated us, even though we had done them no harm, there were also a few who had a more humane attitude. I remember a Carabiniere whose surname was Ferrara, if I'm not mistaken; perhaps he was a friend of the partisans. Well, he brought his fiancée into the camp so that we could agree between us a way to help us escape.

Visits from the outside were very rare, sometimes even undesirable, such as those made by the Blackshirts who came to carry out checks.

There weren't very many of us in the camp and I don't remember many names. Some of them were foreigners who had fled from the horrors of Poland and Germany.

We felt we were at the mercy of events, we had no protection. We were also aware that, as the front line gradually moved, the Germans would take us northwards. There was an elderly English Jewess in the camp who felt more protected than us Italians because she was English.

One morning in late April trucks arrived to take us away. Over those months in the camp I remember there were two marshals who alternated at the Command post. One was tall and sturdily built and the other one, who had a black moustache, we named him Hitler. After the Liberation "Hitler" was put on trial, but my father went to testify that he had done nothing bad to us.

Filippo Ieranò

My mother begged the marshal who was on duty at the time to do something. Well, he had the idea of asking the Germans for the list of names of people who were going to be taken away. They didn't have any documentation so the marshal asked them to return with some written authorisation. It was this that saved us! We realised that if we wanted to save ourselves we had to try to escape. My brother had managed to get in contact with the Allied ex-prisoners. As a matter of fact, once, when he was going to a peasant's house to ask for food, he came across one of them. My brother managed to divert the attention of the Carabiniere who was accompanying him and asked the soldier if anything could be done to help us escape. Using radio transmitters, the former prisoners contacted the Allies. On the night of 3 May, having discovered that the Germans were about to arrive to take us away and being unable to warn us, the Allies bombarded the camp, aiming to demolish the boundary wall.

We often heard Allied planes in the skies above Servigliano; they were probably going to drop bombs on the North and on Germany. That night the noise was the same, but we were amazed at how low the planes were flying. They began to circle above the camp, perhaps to get a good view of the area. We were gripped by fear because we didn't know if they were German planes that had come to kill us or Allied planes that were trying to save us. It had been agreed that they had to hit the perimeter wall.

As soon as the bombs fell the Carabinieri guards closed the entry gate and ran away. At the same time a prisoner from Tripoli jumped over the wall; he managed to open the front gate and let us out. There were a few dozen of us and we all took to our heels in flight. My father had remembered that the river Tenna wasn't far away. He told us to follow him to try to cross the bridge and get to the other side. There were four of us – my mother, father, brother and I – but we couldn't find the bridge, it wasn't there anymore. So we decided to hide in the scrub by the river for the night, where we met also other prisoners.

In the meantime, the planes had gone.

My father knew a local doctor. I don't know whether he was the municipal doctor or just a displaced person who was passing through. I don't remember his name, but he had two daughters. It was this doctor who welcomed us into his house the following morning.

We had just one suitcase with our personal possessions, which had been left in the camp. My father wanted to go and try to recover it and, despite my mother's objection, he cautiously approached the camp, accompanied by my brother. They noticed the effects of the bombing and saw a Carabiniere lieutenant outside the camp. He must have understood everything because he let them enter and then, with an emphatic gesture, he suggested that they get away from there as soon as possible.

Meanwhile other Carabinieri asked us Jewish prisoners to get together in the square. The doctor who wanted to help us, while pretending that nothing was going on, suggested we leave the village. Instead, other Jewish people, broken by so many ordeals and by now exhausted and incapable of lasting out any longer, decided to obey orders. They met up in Servigliano square, in plain view. These were families and old people who would not have been able to escape without help.

I and my family walked off into the countryside, pretending to go for a stroll. As soon as we were away from spying eyes a truck sent by the doctor arrived and took us to the station of a nearby village, where we were advised to catch the first train for Fermo.

At about midday we were waiting for the train, alone with our suitcase, when some way away we saw a girl pedalling quickly down the lane towards us: it was the doctor's daughter. As soon as she reached us, all out of breath, she let us know that the Germans had arrived at Servigliano and were loading the other Jews on to lorries and that they were looking for us. She warned us to hide immediately in the fields.

There were four of us, not just a single person, therefore it was easy to spot us. So we took the girl's advice to go into the fields and wait. While we were hiding, a cart drawn by oxen passed by on the track and the farmer driving it signalled to us to follow him. I believe he had been tipped off by our friend the doctor. We crouched on top of the cart and I remember the sense of unreality that struck me as a 12-year-old: rather than actually living, it seemed as if I was watching a film. After riding a little way we reached a house where we were welcomed and hidden in a room. However, so as to stay together, we went into the stable which was very large.

The next morning the farmer, who was obviously anxious, told my father that we should get away as soon as possible because it was very dangerous. He had gone into the village at dawn and seen that everything was in turmoil because the Germans were searching precisely for us: we were among the few Jews still at liberty. Our hosts were also worried because they had two sons

216

evading military call-up and they feared the risk of them being discovered if there were checks.

However, as there was danger, they made us stay hidden until evening. A car arrived in late afternoon that took us to Fermo, perhaps thanks to the doctor. I think that my brother had already made telephone contact there with a partisan named Ferroni, who was soon to die. He put us in touch with a radiologist at Fermo, Dr. Tomassetti, who was linked to the partisans and with Father Galli of the church of St. Francis. In a few minutes, and before curfew began, we arrived at the church.

Father Galli greeted us warmly but things weren't easy for them either. At the convent they were already looking after a Jew who slept somewhere else at night; then there was a partisan commander condemned to death who was being hunted; and, worst of all, the German headquarters were right on their doorstep.

I remember that one friar, upon seeing us, said: "What, more people? We are in cloisters here!"

But Father Galli replied that it was a question of saving lives and that it was right to do this.

We spent the night at the convent, with my father wide awake and constantly repeating: "I'm going to hand myself in. I've done nothing wrong and I can't stay in hiding. I'm going to get arrested."

Father Galli told him: "Listen, I'm a man of the cloth and I'm telling you that you must save your family. You must go on hiding for their sake, don't be stupid! If you hand yourself in they will take your family too!"

I was sitting on the bed and before my eyes I can still see my father repeating: "I'm going to hand myself in. I've done nothing wrong and I can't stay in hiding. I'm going to get arrested." He was so upset.

In those moments I saw the tensions between two people of different religions: the desperation of my father and the courage of Father Galli.

Luckily my father became convinced. However, it was obvious that it was too dangerous to stay and fortunately Father Galli found a different solution. He remembered that a teacher, named Fortunati, had left an apartment not far from the convent because he was afraid of the bombing and had opted instead to go to a house in the country. We stayed in hiding there until the Allies arrived. I don't recall who brought us the food that we needed, but I do remember that Fortunati had let us stay on one condition: he wanted us always to keep fresh flowers in front of the photo of his late wife. To carry out this task, one day my father and I went during daylight to pick flowers at Villa Vitali. It was incredibly hot and there was nobody about on the roads. But at a certain moment we heard the sound of a bicycle: it was the Carabinieri marshal who had arrested us at Porto San Giorgio. It seemed as if the world had come tumbling down around us. However, he passed by us slowly and proceeded onwards. It's hard to say whether he pretended not to know us or whether he genuinely did not recognise us. Anyway, the fact is that he ignored us.

One day, at last, we watched from the house as the German troops withdrew and immediately afterwards the Allies arrived. Everybody was happy and relieved. Fortunati and his family returned home, even though there was some anxiety because one could still hear shooting a little to the north and people were frightened that the Germans might return. But that didn't happen. And we found somewhere to live.

Things went well for my family.

Most of the other Jews who had been with us in Servigliano camp were not so fortunate. The Germans deported them first to the camp at Fossoli, near Modena, and then to German camps where they were exterminated.

Few were saved. Days later we met up again with a Yugoslav Jewish dentist and his wife at Fermo. Years later we also met a Polish Jew again, at Venice: we knew that Cremeneschi, an engineer, had been helped by the landlady at the house where he had been interned. It appears that as soon as this lady knew about the escape from the camp she went to pick him up in a car and kept him hidden. Another Jew, a woman, was rescued because she had been in hospital at Montegiorgio where there was a doctor who had also tried to help us. When the Germans came to take her she threw herself out of a window, fracturing a foot. Because of this, and at the insistence of the doctor, she was again hospitalised and succeeded in avoiding deportation.

We were lucky but we owe a debt of thanks for having survived: first of all to the Allies who bombed the camp, enabling us to flee; also to the partisans as well as to ordinary people like that doctor at Servigliano who advised us to run off; and to Father Galli and the friars.

We maintained close links with these generous and courageous people. Father Galli attended my wedding. My parents stayed in touch with Fortunati for some years and recently the teacher's daughter tracked me down and we spoke on the phone. But few people, certainly only a few, showed solidarity with us compared with the many who knew of our situation and were indifferent.

There are times when it seems to me as if it was a chapter in fiction, but the more time goes by I realise that it was horribly true. When I was in the camp I often asked myself what we had done, what crime we had committed to deserve such suffering.

When, after the introduction of the racial laws, I was chucked out of school (in the state schools I was able to attend only the first year of elementary school and my brother the first year of secondary school). I always asked the reason. What had we done? And the more that time goes by the more I ask myself what all this was about. The parents of our former school fellows should have told their children what was happening; they should have asked themselves questions and not isolated us, not excluded us. I remember my father's unhappiness when he was put out of his job. He had been a surveyor at Genio Civile [Ministry of Public Works] in Venice. We certainly weren't rich.

But, quite apart from the injustice of the law, my father was hurt by the attitude of everybody who suddenly and for no reason avoided him; it actually affected his health. We're talking about the majority! Then, luckily, there were others who still gave the impression of being a human being: I remember my mother spoke of occasional meetings with the headmaster of the secondary school that my brother attended. He always asked: "What's my boy doing, how is he getting on?"

For these reasons I maintain that it is important to know the true historical facts and to record them; to recall what happened and not misrepresent them.

And yet, after all these years, some time ago I happened to pick up the phone and hear the words "dirty Jew". I couldn't move, I was incapable of replying, I felt the tears slide down my face. I was shocked! It seemed impossible to me that, after everything that had happened, somebody could use the same offensive and unjust words that I had heard years earlier.

I was left with the feeling that everything that had happened had accounted for nothing.

To avoid the same horrors, we must remember.

From a conversation with Carla Viterbo; Verona, September 2001